BE ALWAYS LITTLE

CHRISTIAN FABLES FOR YOUNG AND OLD

BY JUDE FISCHER

MADONNA HOUSE   PUBLICATIONS
Combermere, Ontario   Canada   K0J 1L0

New Edition 1996
Printed and bound in Canada

Illustrations:
Jude Fischer
Daniel Fischer
Fr. Ron Cafeo

Canadian Cataloguing in Publication Data
Fischer, Jude
BE ALWAYS LITTLE
Christian Fables for Young and Old

ISBN 0-921440-26-X

1. Devotional literature 2. Christian life 3. Short stories 1. Title

BV4515.2.F48 1991242C92-090017-8

To my Madonna House family

"Anyone who does not welcome the kingdom of God like a little child will never enter it."
Mark 10:15

Table of Contents

PART 1
Stories by Jude Fischer

PART 2
More Stories by Jude

PART 3
Stories Adapted from Elizabeth York

PART 4
Stories by Daniel Fischer

Poem by Elsie Fischer

Foreword

When I was a child I was fascinated with the imaginative tales my father would weave, giving each of us children a prominent part in the story. And mother would read to us from children's classics and tell us Bible stories. But the stories in this little volume were fathered more than anyone else by Fr. Eddie Doherty, co-founder of Madonna House and first editor of *Restoration*, the Madonna House monthly newspaper. Shortly after his death in 1975 I was standing by his grave unburdening my heart to him. Not long after, his reply seemed to come in the form of a few stories born in my heart. I showed them to Catherine Doherty, the foundress of Madonna House, and she passed them on to Fr. John Callahan with the note "These are really little gems—how about for *Restoration*?" Fr. Callahan in turn printed them in *Restoration* under the heading "Fables." Both of them encouraged me to keep writing, and more stories followed.

Later Catherine urged me to collect them and try to get them published. This little book is in response to that request. The title is taken from a line of the "Little Mandate" given to Catherine: "Little—be always little! Be simple, poor, childlike."

Many readers of *Restoration* had also asked that they be made available in collected form. They wrote telling how they had been touched by this story or that, and shared how they used the tales in storytelling, drama, and puppet shows with children, as well as in retreats with adults. Several readers suggested adding a Scripture text relating to each story, and this has been done as well. Of course, there are many other passages that might come to mind.

This book is divided into four parts. My own stories appear in parts one and two. The first section contains a variety of tales of children, animals, songs, stars, trees, and simple objects of everyday life. The second group of stories revolve around events recorded in Scripture. The delightful stories in the third part are not my own, but were originally told by Elizabeth Rowena Marietta York, a crippled orphan girl, and later published in *Story-Tel Lib* by Annie Trumbull Slosson, Charles Scribner's Sons, 1900. They have since fallen into the public domain and I have adapted them from their original dialect form to the version appearing here. Part four consists of two stories written and illustrated by my brother Daniel Fischer before his death from cystic fibrosis in 1983. And finally, there is a poem written by my mother who died in 1990, on the sacramentality of little things done well.

My gratitude to all who provided seeds for the stories, encouragement, suggestions, and help in getting the book ready for publication. And my prayers for each of you, dear readers. One of the favorite prayers of Catherine Doherty was "Lord, give me the heart of a child, and the awesome courage to live it out." This I pray for all of us. May He lead us to that littleness that fits so well with His greatness.

PART 1

THE BOY AND HIS SONG

ONCE there was a boy. One day when he was out in the fields enjoying the splendor of the flowers and the caress of the breeze, he heard a song—a beautiful song. He stopped and was still, listening. Never had he heard such a beautiful song. He took it to his heart. How happy he was! He loved to listen to the song. He listened while he worked and he listened while he played. He loved to lie on the grass and look into the depths of the blue sky and just listen. And always, wherever he went, whatever he did, he would listen to that song.

He didn't often talk about that song, but on rare occasions he would share it with someone. One day as he did so, the other person sat back and laughed, and laughed, and laughed. "You call that beautiful!? Why kid, you haven't heard anything. Why, I've travelled far and wide, and I tell you there are many better songs than that."

Boy was devastated. His world slowly crashed in on him. What could he do? He loved his song. Yet he was driven to search for the most beautiful song in the world.

So one day he packed his bag and off he went. He hadn't journeyed long when he came to the first song. It was nice. But when he compared it to the song in his heart it paled to nothingness. He continued on his way.

A few days later he came upon another song. It was new and different. It delighted him at first, but when he stopped to listen to the song in his heart, he knew it was but a phantom. So he continued on.

2

He came at last to the sea and sailed across it. Here he found other songs, charming songs, enticing songs, fascinating songs, splendid songs. But their enchantment each in turn faded.

He continued his search over other seas, up mountains, down valleys, through forests, and across wide-open spaces. And as he listened to other songs, the song in his heart grew softer and softer. This was so gradual that he didn't notice it at first. But one day as he went to compare a new song to the one in his heart, he found it so faint that he had to listen very hard indeed to discern it at all. This frightened him at first, but then, he was in a noisy city, and so he attributed it to all the din around him.

Some days later it happened again. He went to listen to the song in his heart, and though he listened very hard, he could hear only one small fragment. This time he wasn't in the city at all, but in a quiet mountain village. He was afraid to think what this might mean. He journeyed on relentlessly, searching, searching. He seldom compared a song to the one in his heart now, because he usually knew ahead of time they wouldn't measure up; and besides, he was afraid.

But one day he thought he would try one last time. He listened for the song in his heart. He listened and listened—but it wasn't there. There was nothing there. Alas! He had travelled everywhere, heard every song, and never found a better one. Not only had he not found a better song, he had lost the one he had. Now he had nothing.

He lay down and sobbed, and sobbed, and sobbed until there were no more tears left in him. Then he lay still, empty. And all was silent. Then out of the silence came a sound, a note, barely heard, almost imperceptible. From within his heart came an answering chord. This was followed by another note, and another, and another, until there it was, the song in his heart. And from that moment on he treasured it carefully and never looked for another.

The Lord is my strength and my song.

–Psalm 118:14

THE ORPHANED MOMENT

ONCE upon a flash of a sparkle, a moment was born. It burst forth into being with all the radiance of its new-found life. It glistened and glowed and delighted in the beauty of being. Then it went forth to join the other newborn moments in the celestial nursery. There, as exciting as simply being was, more adventure was in store for them. For the time had come when each would be appointed his mission in life.

Moment waited eagerly as he heard the others receive their mission. "You are to be a great moment in history," one was told. And another, "You are to be a moment of healing for one in need." And still a third, "You are to be a moment of hope for one despairing." Moment listened earnestly to all this. How splendid it all sounded. He could hardly wait to hear his own appointed destiny.

Finally his turn came! He stepped proudly before the mission-giver, alert for the coming words. The mission-giver looked at him and said, "Go forth, and be lived." Taken aback, moment tried hard to hide his disappointment. He had expected something more, something glorious. But this? "Go forth and be lived?" Of course he'd be lived, a hundred, yes, a thousand times over and more, by everyone he met. There must be something more. He waited to hear it, but the mission-giver had already moved on to the others.

There was nothing to be done. So he plunged down to earth. He'd quickly fulfill this absurdly simple mission.

Then maybe he'd be entrusted with something more challenging. So off he went.

He entered a town and saw a school. Here he'd be lived, then he'd be ready for a greater mission. He bounced cheerily through an open classroom window and went up to an attractive-looking girl. But the girl didn't pay any attention to him. She wasn't paying any attention to the teacher either, for she was too busy thinking of the games she would play when school was over. So moment moved on to the boy in the next seat. He didn't notice moment either, for he was too busy wishing he were older so he could get a job like his brother.

Disappointed, moment left the classroom. Before long he came upon a young man and waved excitedly at him. But the young man seemed not to see him at all. He kept muttering something about how things would be better when he married and found someone to love him.

Next he saw an old man, and approached him with anticipation. "Here I'll find wisdom," he thought. "Here I'll be lived to the full." But the old man ignored him and went rambling on about the good old days. Moment was bewildered by this unexpected response. What to do next? He had to do something to call attention to himself. He turned his questing gaze on the old lady in the next room and tapped her on the shoulder. She too ignored him as she stood before a mirror covering her wrinkles in an effort to look young again.

Next he knocked loudly on the door of a woman with a roomful of children. She opened it, then immediately slammed it in his face. "Go away, I've no time to live you now," she said. "When the kids are raised I'll be able to start living."

Poor moment! He was getting more and more discouraged. Why, it wasn't so simple to be lived after all!

He went from person to person seeking someone to live him, all to no avail. What to do? He thought and thought. How could he get their attention? "I'll come softly in the stillness of the morning, before they are burdened with the cares of the day," he thought. "And beauty. Beauty will do it. I'll come gently with the morning dew, upon the barely opening buds, and let this beauty open hearts for me to enter." So early the next morning he saw a young man, and drew gently near with the dew upon the barely opening blossoms, waiting for the man's heart to open. But the man seemed blind to it all as he sat regretting the mistakes of his past, wishing he could live his life over.

Spring passed, and summer too. Winter came, and still poor moment had not been lived. "I must try something more spectacular," he thought. And so he dressed himself up in a million sparkling snow jewels, and as the sun shone brightly upon him he danced a joyous dance and sang a joyous song before the next person he met. But the young woman he wooed so didn't notice his amazing beauty at all, for her head was filled with thoughts of spring and the crocuses blooming again.

"I know," he thought. "I'll come on the heels of Orion as that mighty giant marches through the sky. They can't ignore the shouting of the brightest stars." But head down, cursing the snow at his feet, the next man to appear never even looked up. He walked along regretting all he hadn't done that day, and worrying about all he had to do tomorrow.

Poor moment! He didn't know what else to do. He had tried everything he could think of, and approached everyone in town. He hung his head, shame penetrating him through and through. How could he return to his mission-giver, having failed in such a simple mission? He trudged slowly away, wondering what he would say. After

walking awhile, he felt someone come up behind him and tap him on the shoulder. He turned to see who it was, but saw no one. But as he looked back at the town that hadn't received him, he noticed smoke rising from a chimney. Funny he hadn't noticed that little cottage before, hidden in the trees. Off he went for this one last chance, knowing it would be fruitless. But he had to try.

There at the side of the cottage was a man chopping wood. The man smiled at him and seemed to beckon him to come and chop wood with him, wood to warm his family, and from time to time he paused a bit from his labor to look at moment and take in each sparkling jewel of his beauty. Then moment entered the house and saw a woman cooking. "Come and warm yourself by the stove," she said, "and be a moment for me to fix this meal for my family." From there moment went into the next room and there was a maiden who invited him to her game of hide and seek with a toddler who laughed with delight at seeing the faces appear and disappear.

Moment was breathtaken. He'd been lived, thrice-fold lived! In his excitement he started to fly back to the mission-giver. "Wait," they called to him. "Don't go yet. Stay with us awhile, we're just beginning to live you. We need you for so much." And so he stayed.

Behold now is the acceptable time,
now is the day of salvation.
                                    –2 Cor. 6:2

THE CHAIR AND THE
FURNITURE DOCTOR

ONCE there was a chair, an ugly scuffy beat-up chair. An uglier, more beat-up chair you never did see. His paint was all chipped and peeling, his colors faded and dingy. There were dents and scratches, unsightly marks and spots, loose legs, a broken rung. Poor chair! He couldn't stand himself anymore. Every year he had gotten uglier and uglier. He couldn't remember that he had ever looked nice really. One coat of paint after another, that was all his life had been. He looked so terrible that people would say, "Let's cover all that ugliness over."

With a fresh coat of paint he'd look better for awhile, but then the paint would start to chip off making him look worse than before, so on went another coat of paint. Then the same thing would happen all over again. So it was black over red over blue over green over white over yellow, layer after layer built up on him. Poor chair, he had forgotten what he was like underneath.

Then one day he found himself in the hands of the furniture doctor. He couldn't tell you how he got there exactly, for it was all so bewildering, a lot of hustle and bustle, some kind of journey on a truck, and there he was. He didn't pay much attention anyway, for he had been around, so many places, and it was always more of the same. He was tolerated as serving a function, but despised for his lack of comeliness, his ugliness.

Now furniture doctor took chair and washed him gently. There was something about his touch that stopped chair for a minute, puzzling him. But he shrugged it off and braced himself for another coat of paint. To his surprise it didn't come. Instead the furniture doctor started scraping the paint away. Ouch! That hurt! Yet there was healing in those hands that hurt.

Patiently the furniture doctor went through layer after layer, and as he worked he sang to the chair:

The   fur - ni - ture doc - tor knows you   chair,

Knows the   beau-ty   that   is   there,

Knows you're not be - yond   re   -   pair,

With some   lov - ing   ten - der   care.

The song soothed chair a bit. Yet with his raw quivering surface he didn't know what to think. What was happening? Why, if anything, he looked uglier than before, with portions of all six layers exposed, each clashing with the others. "I can't stand it," he screamed. "Stop it, cover me over, leave me alone!" But day after day the furniture doctor persisted. Oh, sometimes he gave chair a rest for a few days, and chair was relieved, though he was terribly self-conscious in his half-exposed state. Yet the furniture doctor's shop was just sheltered enough from the onslaught of critical onlookers that chair was able to endure it.

And painstakingly the furniture doctor scraped away through black, red, blue, green, white...

Now chair sensed some change in furniture doctor's touch. Always gentle, always careful, he was now still more so, as if afraid of hurting something. As the last coat of paint, the yellow, began to fall away, chair caught the first breathtaking glimpse of what he was underneath—not paint at all, but wood, beautiful wood. Now chair began to understand what furniture doctor was doing, and why his touch had changed so. Having reached the last layer, he didn't want to scratch or mar the beautiful wood he was about to expose.

Chair eagerly awaited seeing more of himself. Little by little it appeared. Finally he was down to bare wood all over. What a glorious sensation! He reveled in it. He sang and danced a joyous dance. And in his joy he left the furniture doctor, for freed of his bonds of paint, free to be himself at last, he didn't need him anymore. Life was new and exciting, and for the first time in his life he felt in harmony with the world around him.

Then gradually his cloud of glory dissipated a little. He began to settle down. Sometimes he came back and watched the furniture doctor at work. He saw many chairs, tables, desks, pass through the furniture doctor's hands, restored by him to their original radiance. And it seemed to chair that often they began to reflect the beauty of the furniture doctor himself. He began to suspect that maybe he wasn't all he was meant to be. Funny how he hadn't noticed before how rough and dull his wood really was.

He started spending more time with the furniture doctor. Instead of occupying himself with a million other things, he would sit near the furniture doctor all day and keep his eyes on him. One day the furniture doctor said to him, "I think you're ready now." And he came over and started rubbing him with something rough called sandpaper. Ouch! It hurt, but this time chair was sure furniture doctor knew what he was doing. The furniture doctor rubbed and rubbed, then he got some finer paper and the rubbing didn't hurt quite so much. Then some finer paper still, and ah! This time it was nice, never had he had such a nice massage.

Then he rubbed on a strange substance that brought out all the warmth and beauty of the wood and gave him a fine satin smooth finish. Never had chair dreamed he could be so beautiful. He was so proud of himself he called a passer-by to sit on him. And with that, chair nearly collapsed, so wobbly he was! So taken up was he in that beautiful wood that was his, he had forgotten his loose legs! Dismayed, back to the furniture doctor he went. The furniture doctor let him wait around awhile to experience how weak he really was. Then he glued him solidly together, giving some of his strength to chair. And the broken rung he mended too.

Gratefully chair went away. At last he was whole, sturdy, and beautiful. At last he could go forth on his own.

Some days later he looked at himself. He saw a few scratches here, a bit of dust there, a marred area elsewhere. Suddenly he felt an old fear surface—how long would it be until someone came along and covered him again with a coat of paint? He struggled with despair. But then he stopped long enough to look at the furniture doctor. Suddenly he realized clearly what he had long had a glimmer of. He needed the furniture doctor—not just to fix him up once—but he needed the furniture doctor always. He had come from the furniture doctor, he was restored through the furniture doctor, and only through the furniture doctor would he continue to remain and to grow in beauty. He needed him to dust him off, to polish him up, to sand him now and then, to be his strength. Yes, he was never meant to live a life independent of the furniture doctor. Everyday he needed to look to the furniture doctor, and then he didn't have to worry about those coats of paint.

After you have suffered for a little while, the God of all grace will himself restore you, and make you strong, firm and steadfast.   −1 Peter 5:10

THE CHIPMUNK
THAT WENT TO SEA

ONCE there was a chipmunk who lived not far from the sea. He was a shy little fellow, and often he would be seen popping his head out of his hole, carefully looking around to see if it was safe to come out. Sometimes he would bravely come out, only to go dashing back in when he heard some strange feet approaching. But as long as all was well, ah, how he enjoyed life, scurrying around stone walls and brushy rock piles, dashing through the leaves, running from tree to tree, feasting on seeds and nuts. Life was good.

He would have gone on to live his life as any other chipmunk, but for one thing. He had a strange fascination for the sea. It was this more than anything else that would bring him out of his hole in his more timid moments. He would sit by the sea for hours on end just looking at it. Month after month, year after year he did this. Occasionally another chipmunk would catch him at this—rather odd, they thought, yet they tolerated this one idiosyncrasy.

Then one day chipmunk did a very strange thing indeed. He jumped into the sea! He could never tell you why he did this—just that he was overcome by an irresistible urge, and before he knew it, there he was in the water, swimming along as if he had been born in the sea. Such bliss he had never known. It was glorious.

From then on chipmunk went for a swim everyday. One day another chipmunk saw him. The news spread quickly. This was too much. Looking at the sea was one thing, but going into it—unheard of! Absurd! Never had such a foolish thing been done. This must be stopped at once! "You're a chipmunk, not a fish," they said. "You were made for solid ground." Poor chipmunk had no arguments. They sounded so right. Yet he had been in the sea, and he *had* been able to swim. How could he swim if he wasn't meant for the sea?

Days passed with this pull between land and sea. "Stop that nonsense," the other chipmunks said. "Come," said the sea. Finally chipmunk had to choose once and for all. The strange call of the sea won out. Chipmunk said goodbye to his friends and jumped into the sea to stay.

For awhile it was very nice indeed. He was relieved to have made his decision. The embrace of the sea was a joy beyond describing.

But as time went on all this changed. There were storms at sea, and these frightened him. The unknown frightened him even more. He didn't know what lurked in the depths of the sea, and he didn't know the ways of her creatures. He felt more insecure than he ever had before. The other chipmunks must be right. He belonged on solid ground; he was never made for the sea. He couldn't even swim very well, really. How could he ever have delighted in such awkward, ungainly floundering?

On occasion he heard wise fish elders speak to their followers. Surely he was out of his element, for what he heard was certainly beyond the likes of him. How could he have made such an utterly foolish and mad mistake as jumping into the sea? How strong was the pull of the land where he knew the holes, the rock piles, the trees. There were dangers, yes, but he knew what they were and was prepared for them. He belonged on land. He was secure there.

But here in the sea all was unknown. Everything was so strange. He struggled for months with his doubts and confusion. He would have left, but the sea whispered, "Stay, stay." And no matter how great the storm within him, he couldn't deny that voice. And so he stayed.

One day he woke up feeling rather strange. Something was happening in him, but he couldn't say what. He felt better somehow—more quiet inside. And there was the whisper of the sea, "Don't be afraid, I am with you." In this new-found silence, chipmunk lived. He had nothing much to say to the other fish. Other fish! Funny, he was beginning to think like he was one of them. And he was beginning to learn things from them, and beginning to learn things from the sea.

Finally one day he realized the truth in the depth of his being. "I belong to the sea, I really belong to the sea, it's true! I'm supposed to be here." And he grew to love this new element so much and so prospered in it that he had no desire ever again to leave it.

Do not be afraid, for I have redeemed you.
I have called you by name, you are mine.
Should you pass through the sea, I will be
with you; or through rivers, they will not
swallow you up.   —Isaiah 43:1-2

BORN TO SERVE

ONCE upon a time a bowl was born. It wasn't much of a birth. There were no long months of planning for his coming, no excited anticipation of what he would be like, no patient shaping under loving hands, nothing. Scarcely a thought had gone into his design, and as few moments as possible into his making. The quick impersonal movement of a few machines, a trip through a hot oven, and there he was. Nothing much to look at, no warmth, no beauty.

Then he sat in a store and was soon bought, not for his looks, but because he was cheap and would serve a purpose. That he did well. Meal after meal, day after day he faithfully served. For that was his call, to be a simple serving bowl. And all the while no one ever took much notice of him. Sometimes after a meal he would sit around dirty for a long time waiting to be cleaned. Invariably he would be among the last of the dishes to be washed, for the pretty delicate ones always went first. By the time his turn came the water would be rather dirty and cold and it was quite unpleasant really. The girl washing him would mumble and grumble the whole time about this unwelcome chore. The poor bowl bore it all so as to be able to serve once more. And so his life went, meal after meal, week after week, year after year.

Then one day his mistress walked in with a shiny new bowl. It had such a pretty floral design. "Just what I've always wanted," she said. "You'll serve us well and be lovely to look at at the same time." So the first bowl was

packed up with a few other discarded items and sent away. It was a long journey and so tiresome the bowl fell fast asleep. When he woke up much later he found himself in unfamiliar hands. He was plunged into some nice sudsy water and washed up. This bath was quite different from any he had known, and for the first time in his life he actually enjoyed it. It was so refreshing. The water was clean and warm, and the girl washing him didn't seem to mind the task at all, in fact she hummed a merry tune all the while.

Then he was taken to a nice log building. A gift shop, it was called. A very special gift shop. Everything sitting on the shelves waiting to be sold had been donated, and all the money from their sale was given to the poor. When he learned this the bowl became quite excited. He really wanted to help some poor person by his sale. He sat there waiting for his chance, waiting for someone to buy him. But no one did.

No one looked twice at him. For he was so plain, so ordinary, lacking the most elementary charm and grace, and he was surrounded by so many lovely things. Why, the vase next to him was truly exquisite. Just looking at it one could see the love that went into its creation. It must have been carried in the mind of its maker for a long time, tenderly brooded over as its design was perfected down to the last wee detail. Then it was fashioned slowly, painstakingly, under a pair of warm gentle hands, and delicately painted with soft loving strokes. All the time and attention lavished on its creation shone splendidly from its being and drew the attention of all who walked in. It wasn't long at all until it was sold and its sale brought a handsome price to help many. Then there was that little dancing figurine whose presence echoed the joy of its maker, and one could sense that sacred time when sheer goodness flowed from the fingers of its maker and came to dwell in this delightful object.

But as we said, poor bowl knew no such grace or beauty. Repeatedly overlooked, he nearly gave up all hope of being sold. He settled into life in the shop. It wasn't bad really. He enjoyed the care and attention paid him by those who worked there even if no one else took a second glance at him. He was dusted regularly and he liked the warm touch of the hands that held him so gently as they did this. Often he was moved around from shelf to shelf, given new companions, and every effort was made to display him as nicely as possible even though it seemed to no avail. After he had been there a long time he was given another nice warm sudsy bath. He was quite content with all this for awhile.

But after a number of years he grew rather wistful. This unexpected retirement had been very nice, but after all, he had been born to serve, and he knew in his heart it was time to get on with his life of service. But still he waited. Then one day he heard the people at work in the shop talk about a little boy who needed a wheelchair, but had no money for it. The next sales in the shop would supply it for him. Bowl's heart jumped. How he would love to help the boy—and get back into service as well. But what could he do? No one ever looked twice at him.

Then he heard a woman walking toward him. He knew her attention would go immediately to that attractive tray at his right, or the elegant silver teapot to his left. But she looked right at him, smiled, and said, "Just what I'm looking for, just like grandmother used to have. So lovely, and you'll do a nice job of serving my family as well." Lovely?! He'd never been called that before. Serve them well, yes, he would. But be lovely? Never. He knew better than that.

She picked him up and walked to the counter to pay for him. On the way they passed a mirror. The bowl looked in and was amazed. For he was indeed lovely. Much the same, and yet so different. Radiant! Why, he positively glowed, and his plain design sparkled warmly. He couldn't believe it! He'd never looked that way before. Then suddenly he recognized that what he was seeing was what he had felt all those times he was so lovingly handled by those girls in the shop as they washed and dusted and arranged him. Their love had clung to him and filled him and subtly transformed him. And now, not only would he begin a life of service again and realize his dream of helping the boy, but from now on he'd give delight by his presence as well.

We, with our unveiled faces reflecting like mirrors the brightness of the Lord, all grow brighter and brighter as we are turned into the image that we reflect.   –2 Cor. 3:18

THE ABANDONED BOX

ONCE there was a box, a cast-off box, sitting in a junkpile. Sadly he thought, "I'm no good, no good at all, old and beat-up by the years, there's no more room for me in this shiny plastic world." He thought of his earlier years when as a young wood box he had proudly held cigars for his master—what joy it had been to present him with one each day. Finally empty, he thought, "What now?"

The master's little son came along and adopted him and made of him, joy of joys, a cache for his treasures—sea shells, butterflies, stones, baseball cards, marbles, pennies. A never ending stream of precious things came and went from him. In the process he got banged here, scratched there, but he didn't really mind, for he loved boy and he loved bearing his treasures.

Then one day boy went away and left box behind. Other children picked him up and put things in him and used him for awhile—but they didn't really care about him the way boy used to. They scratched initials on him and left him out in the rain and spilled ink on him.

Finally one day someone picked him up and threw him in the garbage. What a tragic day that was! Set aside, declared no longer able to be of service to anyone! A big truck picked him up and dumped him in this junkheap where he now found himself. Battered and bruised and cast-off, he was feeling very sorry for himself indeed.

Then one day box-mender came along and picked him up, to box's great surprise. He took box home. Box's heart jumped with anticipation. But then box-mender put him on a shelf and walked away. Days passed and nothing happened. Box's heart sank. Had he been rescued only to be forgotten?

Finally one day when box was sure he could bear it no longer, box-mender picked him up again. He dusted him off and washed him clean. He bleached out his stains, but not all of them. He sanded out his scratches, but not all of them. "You will carry some of your scars within you," he said to box, "so that you will be sensitive to the wounds of others." He covered box with some nice soft cotton padding. And over that he put the prettiest printed fabric that box had ever seen. Box was so overcome with joy, you might have thought he'd be bubbling over, yet so moved was he by this unexpected goodness, so awestruck by the mystery of it all, he stood in silence. And always, as box-mender worked on him, there was healing in that touch.

Finally box was finished. He was given as a gift to a lonely lady, bearing box-mender's love with him. Box was happy in his new home; he knew he cheered up the lady. And he knew also some kind of oneness with box-mender. He knew that no matter what happened to him now, this could always be there. And he knew too, the scars he bore within, and remembering his mender's words, he cherished them for what he was being taught through them.

I have formed you, I will not forget you.
                                           –Isaiah 44:21

THE TREE THAT
COULD NOT SPEAK

ONCE there was a tree in the forest. He was a very silent tree. The other trees whistled in the wind, whispered their secrets one to another, rustled their leaves in the new excitement of each day. But not this tree. He remained silent from the day he first pushed his little head above the ground. His parents waited with eagerness for his first sound. But it never came. As the other little trees chattered away, he alone remained silent. "Why are you so quiet," he was asked again and again. In response he merely wept silently. He didn't know why. He tried again and again to whistle, to whisper, to rustle with the wind, but nothing happened. Sometimes his heart would be so full of what he wanted to share with the others, but when he tried, nothing came forth. For he was just a silent tree, no matter how he tried.

As he grew older, he became familiar with death. A few of the trees lived to a ripe old age, and their life energy spent, peacefully died. But not many. Most were taken young, cut down in the prime of their life, and used to serve man's needs. As tree matured, he began to worry about that. He saw one after another of his peers go. And he was afraid. For what he longed for most of all in life was to speak, to pour out his heart to his fellow trees. Secretly he hoped beyond all hope that someday, somehow, this would happen. And he didn't want to die before it did. He didn't want to die before he had really lived, before he had found his voice. Yet day after day silence remained his companion.

Then one day the woodcutters appeared in the forest again. He saw others of his neighbors felled. Then one woodcutter approached him. He knew it was the end. He wept, bitterly disappointed. His dream would never be realized. He submitted to the axe and was dragged out of the forest.

The next few days were very confusing. There was pain, lots of pain. He lost all of his lovely leaves, and his once graceful form was utterly destroyed as he was cut this way and that. Then came the time when he was set aside in pieces for what seemed a long, long time. Finally one day a young man picked him up gently and started working with him. Tree quivered with anticipation as he was cut, bent, shaped, glued. Sometimes it hurt, yet he sensed something good in the air, and he let the man do as he would with him. And little by little he saw himself take another shape, not like the one he had as a tree, but a beautiful one nonetheless. He had never seen anything quite like it. What did the man call it? Yes, a violin, that was it.

And the young man picked him up and started to play. And poor tree wept with joy. For he was hearing his own voice for the first time, the voice he had given up ever hearing. He was speaking, he was singing, yes, he was pouring out his heart in song. The young man walked with him back into the forest. And he sang to all the trees there, sang and sang. Once, alive in that same forest, he had been silent, but now that he was dead he sang songs. And one of the trees bent down and kissed him.

All the works of the Lord are good, and he will supply every want in due time.   –Sirach 39:33

THE RIVER THAT HATED HER BANKS

ONCE upon a time there was a river—a mighty fine river indeed. There were countless people who loved and enjoyed her. Children sailed their makeshift little boats on her edge, picked her lovely flowers, and waded delightedly as far as they dared go. Some people swam in her, or spent quiet days fishing in her depths. Others rowed miles along her, taking in the breeze and sunshine, the beauty of the foliage that bedecked her edges, and the ever changing reflection of light and color upon her waters. She cooled the hot, watered the thirsty, refreshed the weary, calmed the restless, gave all a welcome change from their humdrum daily life. Indeed, she was loved by all. And so she lived her days, happy and content. She liked watching all her visitors and enjoyed their company.

Then gradually something changed in her, and the river grew restless. She longed to know what lay beyond her banks. So many people came and went from her. She wondered where they went and what they did when they left her. She envied their freedom, their easy coming and going, while she had to stay bound up in her banks. She felt lonely on those quiet days when no one came to her. Weeks passed and her restlessness increased, until she could contain it no longer.

One busy working day when all her friends were gone, she decided to go and see them. So she flooded her banks and travelled merrily along. What joy, what freedom! What

35

new sights she had never seen before! She rambled blithely along, enjoying very minute. Then she came upon one of her friends who had visited her often. She smiled her greeting, but her friend was dismayed, so figuring it was best to leave her friend alone for awhile, the river continued on her way.

She came to another friend, driving his car. Remembering the many happy hours this man had spent in his boat upon her waters, she decided to give him a nice surprise—a little bonus ride—so she made a little turn, floated the car away, then left it stranded in a field. As she left, she heard the driver warning other cars away. "Funny they don't appreciate me," mused the river.

She continued on. A woman screamed something about her garden being destroyed. She entered a house. People snatched things away from her and ran upstairs. She caught a child in her flow, and the child cried out in panic. Why, the child didn't seem to delight in the river's ride at all. Finally a man swam in and grabbed the child and carried her away.

River was bewildered. She had expected her friends to be happy to see her. She had looked forward to new sights and new freedom. But nothing was going right. She grew more and more depressed. Nobody appreciated her. She stopped her flow, and sat around dejectedly in big puddles. Finally she crept back to her bed, happy to see her banks once again. And before long there were her happy smiling friends enjoying her once more.

Little by little she grew to love her banks. And though she still grew restless from time to time, she knew the answer didn't lie in leaving her banks. And so she stayed within them.

Then one morning she woke up and looked at her banks—but they weren't there. She found herself instead in the arms of the sea. What delight in that embrace! What bliss, what rapture! Strange how it was her banks that brought her there.

You were called to freedom. But do not use your freedom as an opportunity for self-indulgence; rather, serve one another in love.   –2 Gal. 5:13

FROM DARKNESS TO LIGHT

ONCE upon a time in the cool dark depths of the earth a diamond was born. He was not at all striking to look at, just a dull crystal, like all the rest of his family, lying in rough stone. Yet hidden in the darkness of the earth, he was content and lived a very peaceful life. As a young diamond he sometimes heard tales of his forefathers, how at some point they had left their earthy home and begun a new life in a place of light. He wondered about this, but somehow found it difficult to imagine. And so he continued his quiet life in the darkness where he grew and matured.

Then one day he heard some noise in the distance. Day by day it grew closer. Sounds of blasting and shouting and digging and disruption of the earth around him. Then bit by bit a passageway was formed that went right by him. He saw a black man at work who seemed weary and coughed a lot in the close suffocating air. His back seemed to bother him. As he got to know the man, the diamond learned he had injured his back when a wall of rock where he was digging had fallen down on him. But that was a long time ago. Now he was mostly worried about his wife and children he had had to leave back in his native village a long way away. He sorely missed them, and had just received news of a drought in the village. His wife helplessly watched the crops wither, her months of labor gone in a few days, and the scraggy cow had ceased to provide milk. And now, on top of it all, the baby was sick. He would be paid tonight and would write to his wife, enclosing his hard-earned wages that would give them a bit extra to eat for a little while. But it was so little, and their needs so great it could hardly begin to meet them. As the diamond learned all this his heart grew heavier and heavier and tears rolled quickly down his cheek.

And then, before he knew it, the diamond felt himself moved out from his secure niche in the earth, torn away from his warm wrapping of kimberlite and carried to the top of the earth. Gradually there was light, then more and more, so dazzling it hurt his eyes, and he was afraid. He crawled back under the piece of kimberlite where he had hidden for so long and sheltered himself there from the light. Sometimes he'd crawl out to the edge for a little while to take a peek at the world of light, but it was too bright. It blinded him, so that he couldn't look for long. He wondered how anyone could live in such a world.

He lay on top of the earth for a long time it seemed, mostly concealing himself under the rock around him, occasionally taking a quick look out. Then one day he was scooped up and carried away, and in the next few days so much happened to him. He was carried here and there, put through this process and that, but all the time he screened himself as much as possible from the light by hiding under his companions on the journey.

One day someone picked him up. It was a beautiful woman. He couldn't take his eyes off her, she was so lovely and infinitely peaceful, and the diamond felt himself filled with a strange new peace just looking at her. She sheltered him from the light in the palm of her hand and said, "You're afraid of the light, aren't you?" Diamond was so relieved that at last he had found someone who understood. "Yes," he said, "I can't live so near the light, I am a child of darkness." She smiled and explained she understood his fears since all he had ever known was darkness, but that he had really been made for the light. And she gently carried him over to where there were two little diamond crystals playing in the light. Laughing and splashing, it looked like so much fun. "Now come," said the lady, "I will give you a bath in the light." She slowly raised her hand that was protecting him from the light and tenderly lifted him to a ray of the sun. How strange it felt, not fearful as he had anticipated, but very pleasant. Then the lady took a handful of light and poured it down his forehead. The diamond felt like he'd been invested a prince! He felt the light flow down his face and envelop his whole body. With delight he splashed it in the air, caught it again, lay down in it, basked in its warmth and brightness, all the time incredibly amazed at the affinity he had for it.

"This is just the beginning," said the lady. "You can not only enjoy the light, but you can reflect its brilliance back to the world. It will hurt a little," she explained. "You will need to be cut this way and that, again and again, but with each cut you will more and more reflect the light you love." So with this explanation, the diamond was not afraid when the lady handed him over to the gemcutter, and though it hurt a little he didn't really mind, for sure enough, with each cut he more and more reflected the light he loved, and his whole being glowed as with fire.

At one point the cutter looked at him through a lens and remarked on his flaws. "Very minor imperfections, most diamonds have them," he said. But they weren't enough to affect his beauty; he was a fine diamond by any standard nonetheless. "Flaws," the expert called them, but the diamond knew they were his tears for the black man and his family that had remained in his heart.

Then he was given a final polish and mounted in a beautiful gold setting to begin his life as a ring. There followed a long journey to a jewelry store where he was put on display and admired by many. One day a woman came into the shop and acclaimed him for his size. "I'll buy it," she said, "it's bigger that the one my neighbor has, won't she be jealous," and with that the diamond shed another tear. He was taken to his new home, full of things to impress visitors, but empty of the peace and love he so longed for.

One day his mistress walked into another shop to buy more things to made her feel important and to impress others. But it was a different kind of shop than any she had visited before. All the beautiful things sitting on the shelves had been donated to help the poor of the world, and all the money from their sale was sent to hungry and hurting people everywhere. The woman found it hard to believe that anyone would give these lovely things away. In fact, the very thought of it irritated her at first. But as she browsed through the shop she gradually sensed a certain peace. And before long she found herself talking of her cares and worries to one of the ladies who worked there. The simplicity and peace and love she met began to penetrate her heart and she felt relieved of a great burden. As she left the shop she saw a box marked "For Christ's poor everywhere." Some strange movement in her heart which she couldn't explain prompted her to take the ring off her finger and drop it in. And as she did so the diamond discovered that one of his tears was wiped away.

Later in the week when the donation box was opened, the shop staff exclaimed in amazement to discover the diamond there and wondered who had left it and why. They gently picked up the diamond, lovingly cleaned him, and displayed him in a beautiful blue velvet box where he seemed even more brilliant than before. A few days later a young man walked in, full of love for a beautiful young lady. His eyes looked past all the other gems and came to rest on him. "That's the one," he said, excitedly, "the perfect diamond for her, it sparkles like her eyes." Diamond liked him right away and was caught up in his youthful enthusiasm. And the warmth of the young man's love dried another of his tears.

Then he heard the saleslady thank the man for his purchase and tell him where the money would be going. When the diamond heard the sale would help the sick and hungry in a drought stricken village in the country where he was mined, he felt his heart jump with joy and his final tears were wiped away. And now radiant and flawless, he reflected the light more fully than ever before and went happily forth to his new home.

We are all children of light, children of day.
We do not belong to night or darkness.
–1 Thess. 5:5

THE CHAMPION FALLER

ONCE there was a young lad who dreamed of becoming a trapeze artist. From early boyhood he had admired the grace, the ease, the freedom, the faultless performance of these artists of the sky, and longed to join them. Finally the day arrived when at long last he was accepted as a student. What exhilaration was his as he climbed high overhead for the first time.

It didn't prove to be easy though. His instruction wasn't far along when the falls began. He tried and fell, tried and fell again. The first couple of falls weren't bad, but they were only the beginning. With each succeeding fall, his aches and bruises grew. But worse than the bodily pain was the fear he began to experience. He became so preoccupied with the possibility of falling that he could not pay full attention to his teacher, watch his movements, listen to his instruction. And so his falls grew more and more frequent; his fears more and more consumed him.

Finally in one especially disastrous fall, his partner was killed and he himself was so badly bruised he ended up in the hospital for a long time. With so much time on his hands he focused more and more on his wounds, and his despondency grew. He had failed in the only thing he had ever wanted. It was hopeless to think he could ever be a trapeze artist. All he could do was fall and fall again. Champion faller, that's what he was. And he didn't want to be destroyed like his partner. Defeated, he gave up his dream.

Many months later he left the hospital, healed at last. He didn't know what he would do, all he knew was that this trapeze artist business was over, finished. He searched for a new dream. But none captured him.

One day at a friend's urging, he reluctantly visited a circus once again. As he watched the trapeze artists perform, he noticed one who was truly a master. Never had he seen such superb artistry. The old desire stirred in his heart. He tried to push it down, deny it. But it was too strong. This is what he wanted more than anything else, to follow this man, to imitate his movements, his grace, his beauty, to become like him. His fears didn't matter. Nothing mattered but following the master. He remembered his previous failures—how dare he try again? Yet so strong was his desire, so powerful the attraction of the master, that before he knew it he was in front of him saying, "Teach me to be like you."

"Come," said the master, and led him up, up, and up. When they got to the dizzying heights, the young man's fears returned. He shuddered and then stood paralysed. How utterly foolish he'd been to come up to these heights. Finally he turned to the master shamefaced, and admitted his fear.

"Yes, you will fall," said the master. "You will fall and fall again. But don't be afraid, for I am with you and you will not be harmed." The lad wondered how this could be so, yet something in the master instilled confidence in him. And so he resumed his instruction.

And sure enough, it wasn't long before he plunged into another fall. This time from such great heights that surely nothing but disaster could possibly result, shattered bones and crushed spirit. But when he landed it was none of those things. Instead, to his astonishment, he found he was borne up gently by a net, and he got up rejoicing in his master's protection, free now to keep his eyes on his master, free to try and try again and really begin learning.

The Lord supports all who fall and raises all who are bowed down.   –Psalm 145:14

THE LAND THAT
WOULD NOT PLAY

ONCE there was a boy who grew up in Hill Country. He played many games with her, and took a long time getting to know her. For Hill Country took great delight in hiding herself, in revealing herself little by little, bit by bit. The boy would approach a hill, and as he climbed, Hill Country would disappear, but for the top of the hill and a bit of sky. Then as he went over the top, Hill Country would surprise him with a breath-taking view, revealing a part of herself the boy had never seen. This never lasted for long though, for soon boy would be deep in the woods, unable to see even Hill Country's forests for the trees. There was constant change. Hill Country revealed herself in pieces, a lake here, a grove there, now a field, again a cliff, so many different things, and little by little the boy got to know and love Hill Country.

Then one day the boy received an invitation to visit Prairieland. So off he went, very excited. He looked forward to playing games with Prairie, games of hide and seek like he had with Hill Country. But instead of hiding, Prairie stood there wide open for boy to see. The boy was taken aback. Never had the land laid herself so wide open to him before. "How can I find you if you don't hide?" he asked, irritated. But still Prairie stood there wide open. The boy studied her for awhile, then went on his way, but wherever he went it was the same, there Prairie stood, wide open. Finally he'd seen all there was to see of

Prairieland, and was ready to go back to Hill Country, ready to play more games of hide and seek.

The morning of his departure he woke up and looked at Prairieland one last time. He sensed something he hadn't noticed before. There was something awesome about the land, its silence, its defenselessness, its openness. Such a radical openness that boy had never dreamed of. A bits and pieces openness, an occasional brief wider openness he had seen, but nothing like this. He sensed too that Prairieland was not as easily known as she had seemed at first. True, she was wide open, yet she held many subtle secrets, a complex unique selfhood that took long listening to understand.

And as boy stood there looking at Prairie, a slow realization took hold of him. Prairieland was never meant to be his playmate, but his teacher. A silent staretz speaking by her very being. And so boy put aside his games and stayed.

My son, if you wish, you can be taught.
If you are willing to listen, you will
learn.   –Sirach 6:32-33

A Shirt-Tale

ONCE there was a shirt, not an ordinary shirt, but a handsome white shirt, beautifully embroidered with designs of distinction. Ah, a shirt as handsome as he is seldom to be found. He did not belong to any ordinary person, but to a very important man indeed. So, needless to say, he became very proud. How he loved to show off his fineness on his master's daily walks.

Now from time to time this shirt, like every other shirt, found himself in the laundry. He didn't like this very much, but his protests were ignored, and so he came to accept the inevitable. And in the end it was worth it to return to his owner fresh and spotless and ready to display his grandness once again for all to see.

But there was one trip to the laundry that ended differently. He was left to soak for awhile with a common blouse. The blouse's blue ribbon started to run, and left an unsightly blue blotch on the handsome shirt. Shirt looked at himself with horror. He could never return to his master this way, he must be radiantly clean and without stain. The chagrined laundress seemed to agree. She picked him up with concern and compassion in her eyes and said, "This spot must come out!" Shirt fervently agreed.

The laundress had a box of funny looking tubes and bottles and jars and cans with solutions and creams and powders and sprays guaranteed to remove anything. She tried one—nothing happened. She tried another. Nothing happened. A third, and still nothing happened. And so she went through the lot, but the stain was still there. Shirt was terribly dismayed. Another lady came in and said, "Try this, it works every time." The laundress tried it, but it didn't work. So she soaked him some more, first in one solution, then in another, and another. But still nothing happened. Shirt was feeling very sore indeed from all this treatment.

He began to realize his life would never be the same. He could never again be a handsome shirt, worn by a distinguished master. His would be the lot of the common ordinary shirt. He thought he'd be very awkward in this new role, there was a lot he'd have to learn, much he'd have to change in himself. For a long while he kept to himself, but gradually during the long period he spent in the laundry, he began to speak to the other shirts. He was surprised to find they didn't hold his blemish against him. He came to know them, and to know their ways. He even began to like them and care about them. There was a lot more in them that he had ever dreamed of.

Then one day the laundress picked him out of the solution where he was soaking with another shirt, and looked at him resignedly. "Well, I've done everything I can," she said. "The only thing left to do is to turn you over to the sun." And so she took him out and hung him on the line. Shirt shivered. It was so cold out there. Why, his master had never taken him out on cold days without first putting a nice warm jacket over him. How embarrassed he was to have his blemished body exposed to the view of every passer-by. And it was so lonely. All his shirt companions had responded well to other treatments, and he was the only one condemned to hang outside, exposed to cold and shame and ridicule, lonely, unloved, uncared for. The ground was white with snow, and the

only shirts that went by were buried in jackets and so did not see him. His life was barren and desolate.

Then one day as he looked about him he noticed the pale orb of the sun above. And he looked to it. There was something about it that somehow impelled something in him. He couldn't explain it, but somehow he felt a kinship with the sun. He looked at the orb and was comforted somehow, and as he looked, he began to perceive some warmth coming to him through all that cold and sharpness. At night the sun would leave and the shirt would quietly await his return. As the days passed, the sun's rays seemed to get warmer and warmer, so that shirt didn't even notice the cold after awhile. He just spent his days looking to the sun, oblivious of the cold and snow and lack of companions. It was his only consolation.

Then one day the laundress came out. She looked at him and smiled. Her smile reminded him of the warmth of the sun. And she said, "you're white again, white at last." Astonished, the shirt glanced down and saw that it was so, that in those long lonely days of looking to the sun, something had happened. Then he gratefully looked back to the sun who alone had the power to transform him.

Every face turned to him grows brighter.
                                              –Psalm 34:5

Mirabel and the Golden Ring

ONCE upon a time there was a penniless young girl, an orphan. Her mother and father had both died when she was but an infant, and there was some suggestion that her origin was somehow disreputable. So she had heard from as far back as she could remember. She had gone to live with various neighbors and relatives, but was welcome with none of them. Times were hard, and another mouth to feed meant less for everyone else. So she was shuffled back and forth, a few months here, a few months there. When she was old enough she did what she could to help out, but it was never enough to satisfy anyone. Finally she struck out on her own, doing various odd jobs here and there in return for a night's lodging in a barn or a bite to eat. Summers were best, for then she often slept outdoors and lived on nuts and berries and various other wild plants.

No one wanted her. No one bothered much with her. No one, that is, except a rather dreary old man who visited her regularly. He always had, from as far back as she could remember. It was he who had told her of her sad origins, of the untimely death of her parents. And he told her that although she wasn't worth much, he would be there when she needed him. He taught her a little about life and warned her of life's dangers. Often his talk was quite dismal and gloomy, but still, he was available to talk to, and she was so lonesome sometimes.

Life was hard. Winters were long, and she had to work endless hours for a bit of bread and a roof over her head.

Her shabby clothes were faded and patched many times over.

Yet she had one thing that gave her joy. It was a golden ring that she wore on a string around her neck, beneath her clothing. She loved to look at it when it caught the sun's golden rays and shone like a miniature sun itself. It was delicately engraved with birds and flowers which seemed to come alive when the sunlight hit them, delighting her so. And there on the inside of the band was engraved her name, Mirabel. Though she had never been taught to read, she had learned just enough to make out her own name. After her name was an inscription which she couldn't read.

It awed her that she should own something so beautiful. She had never shown it to anyone. Not even the old man with whom she shared so much. Why, she wasn't sure, but there was some hesitation deep within her. Maybe he'd say it was a mistake, it couldn't really be hers. Imagine, an unworthy servant girl with a golden ring! He might insist that they try to find its true owner, or that it be sold to buy much needed food and clothing, or to pay back those who had helped her. Or perhaps he'd even accuse her of stealing it. But she hadn't. Where it had come from she didn't know, but it had been around her neck from as far back as she could remember. And though she didn't know exactly what she feared, she carefully kept the ring hidden beneath her clothes and took it out only when she was alone.

One day in the course of her travels, she came upon a beautiful castle. It glowed in the sunlight and had the loveliest gardens around it the girl had ever seen. After that she walked by the castle often just to drink in its beauty. There were trees laden with delicious fruit, their branches hanging invitingly over the castle walls. How she longed to reach out and take one! But it could never be. For the old man had warned her of the king's jealous watch over the fruit and the terrible punishment that awaited anyone who tried it. One day as she hungrily eyed the fruit, the gatekeeper of the castle saw her and said, "Help yourself to as much as you like." But Mirabel, remembering the old man's warning, politely refused.

She continued her daily walks past the castle just to glimpse through the gates the lovely peaceful gardens. Once the gatekeeper invited her in. She was startled and said, Oh no, she couldn't. Later she mentioned this to the old man. He approved her response, and again warned her never to go into the garden. He explained that the king was a hard and cruel man who reserved the garden exclusively for his family's use and was merciless to anyone who dared enter, especially the likes of her with her humble and questionable background. The gatekeeper had been hired to lure unsuspecting travellers inside. Poor Mirabel shuddered and was glad she hadn't accepted the gateman's offer.

Still, the garden attracted her. One day as she walked by the castle she climbed a tree to get a better look. And she saw the king himself there, walking back and forth within the garden. His eyes seemed so kind and compassionate, yet with some indefinable sadness. She couldn't imagine him harming anyone. But she remembered what the old man had said. She climbed back down the tree and continued her walk around the castle. The gateman greeted her when she approached. "The king is in the garden, wouldn't you like to go in and meet him?" he asked. "Oh, I couldn't," replied Mirabel. Then she ventured to add, "He looks so kind." "He is," said the gateman. Mirabel wondered at this and went on her way. Later the old man again warned her of how heartless the king could be. He

told how many had entered the garden never to return. Such beauty was never meant for nobodies like her.

Still the castle and its garden and the kind-looking king drew her again and again. At least she could look from afar, and that was better than nothing. Then one day she saw children in the garden playing, having a wonderful time. The king was smiling at them, taking the small ones in his lap, walking hand in hand with the others, talking with them about the birds and flowers and animals they saw. How Mirabel longed to be among them. How lonely she felt.

As she walked by the gate the keeper said. "The king is waiting for you. You're his child too, you should be there with the others." Mirabel laughed at such a preposterous line and started to leave. Just then one of the king's daughters came towards the gate. As she came nearer, Mirabel saw a ring on her finger. Why, it was just like hers! In her excitement she pulled out her own ring, then immediately regretted this reckless impulsive act, fearing its consequences. But then the princess's arms were around her in a joyous embrace. "My sister, my joy, we've been waiting so long for you." And then in response to the signal of the gatekeeper, the king and all the other children came running out to meet her, embracing her again and again. There followed a joyous celebration in the garden, and Mirabel, the princess who hadn't known she was a princess, heard how she had disappeared from the castle shortly after her birth and never been found. They read to her the inscription on the ring, "Mirabel, daughter of the King." And the celebration continued.

The Lord brings the counsel of the heathen to nought, but the counsel of the Lord stands forever. —Psalm 33:10

THE STAR THAT FELL
FROM THE SKY

O NCE there was a boy who was in love with the sky.
By day he watched the clouds and sunrise and
sunset. By night the moon and bright shining stars. He
especially delighted in the coolness of the night. Every
evening he looked to the sky and just marvelled at its
grandeur. One night something strange happened. He saw
one of the stars plunge from the sky and descend slowly
toward him. It kept coming, smiling at him, and landed
right at his feet. A gift from the sky! A gift for him! He
was awed and humbled at the sky's goodness to him.

Wherever he went, the star went with him and he knew
the sky's love for him. Even when angry clouds filled the
sky, even when he visited the busy city whose smog hid the
sky from his view and obliterated all trace of the stars, he
looked at his sparkling star and knew the sky's love for
him.

So he passed many years secure in that love. Then one
day a voice said to him, "You are not worthy of the sky.
You are not worthy of his love. That star was never meant
for you." A shadow passed over the boy's heart. He tried
not to listen to the voice, but the voice grew louder. He
looked to the sky, but it seemed dark and foreboding. He
looked to the star, the lovely glistening star, and said "I
guess you were never meant for me." He laid the star
tenderly on the ground and covered it over with soft earth

and put some flowers over it. And then he said a silent goodbye with tears in his heart.

And with that goodbye all the joy went from the boy's life. He could not look to the sky that did not love him, the sky that could not love him since he was not worthy, since he was nobody. How lonely he was! The clouds and the sunset and the stars held no comfort for him.

He went into his house, closed the doors and windows, and tightly pulled all the shades and curtains. He did not want to look at that disapproving sky. He tried to forget his sorrow. How many books he poured through, games he played, hours he slept, so many things he did, to forget, simply to forget. But somehow the pain was still there, year after year.

Sometimes there was a knock at the door. But he never answered. He didn't want to see that somber frowning sky. Finally one day the knocking grew louder, more persistent. Still he ignored it. But this time it kept up, never stopping. Poor boy! What to do? He couldn't read, he couldn't play his games, he couldn't sleep, he couldn't do anything to forget his sorrow with that racket at the door. There was nothing to do but go and answer it. But quickly, for he didn't want to glimpse much of that disapproving sky.

He opened the door. And there dancing and smiling before him was his star. So happy was boy to see the star, he forgot how unworthy he was. He smiled back and danced a joyful dance with the star. And he looked up to the sky which embraced him tenderly. "It was a lie that voice told you," the sky said softly, "the star is my gift to you. You see, I love you so very much."

Behold, I stand at the door and knock; if anyone hears my voice and opens the door, I will come in to him... —Rev.3:20

THE TREE THAT WAS RUINED

O NCE there was a tree. He lived happily in a big forest with many other trees. Occasionally fellow trees were cut down and taken away, and he grieved for them. But then he discovered that his friends had not died forever. Instead, under skilled hands they were reborn into some object for human living. And so when his turn came he was not surprised. What would his new life be, he wondered? A cradle to rock a child to sleep? A table to feed him? It would be wonderful whatever it was. And so he stood up fearlessly to the axe.

Before long a woodcarver came along, examining the fallen trees. He said he was looking for choice trees he could carve into beautiful figures, figures that would live forever, delighting people with their beauty. He chose one tree, then another, then the tree this story is about. This tree was so happy, so very happy to be chosen. It would be better than he'd ever dreamed. How proudly he would stand in the world's finest museum, looked upon by generation after generation as they gazed at his beauty. He looked forward to his new form, his new and exciting life. He jumped with joy as the woodcarver approached him to begin his work. But alas, his jump made the carver's knife slip, and he gouged the tree too deeply in the wrong place. The tree was beyond saving. The form the carver had in mind would never emerge. In fact, the tree wouldn't fit into any of the carver's plans now. And so he moved on to another tree.

Over the next little while various other carvers looked at tree and shook their heads regretfully. "It's a pity," they said. "Such beautiful wood, such exceptionally fine grain, such mellow color. You would have been so fine to work with, but now you're ruined, there's nothing in you now. We should throw you into the fire."

Poor tree wept. He saw such beautiful shapes emerge from the trees around him. What would become of him? Would he alone not live on? Was he no good except to be chopped up and burned? Then he would die and never live forever.

Then one day a new carver appeared in the forest. He walked up to the tree and sat down. He just sat and looked at the tree, saying nothing. Then he went thoughtfully away. The next day he returned. And the next. It was strange, how day after day he came and just sat and looked at the fallen tree. Tree started to look forward to these visits, to that loving gaze, though he felt he dare not say anything until the man spoke first. Day after day the man returned and they simply looked at each other in silence.

Finally one day the man did speak. "I see it now," he said, "I see the shape you were meant to be." And he started to carve. He carved day and night, full of his passion to see the figure come forth. Tree didn't understand what was happening. He'd been told time and time again that he'd been ruined, would never be anything beautiful. But as this new carver continued his work, tree sensed something remarkable happening. He felt new life surge through his being and finally he emerged, a dancer, caught in precisely that singular moment of his dance when he fit exactly the contours of that damaged piece of wood. All who came marvelled at this masterpiece, more alive than any carving done before. Some said the flaw forced the artist to be more inventive and original than he ever would have been with more perfect materials. I don't know. But the tree reborn a dancer, danced away to the delight of all who came by.

We know that by turning everything to their good God cooperates with all those who love him, with all those he has called according to his purpose.
—Romans 8:28

THE CAVE THAT
WAS FULL OF ITSELF

ONCE upon a time there was a cave. There was a bear who used to visit the cave. In fact, the bear loved to go to the cave and the cave loved to have him come. The bear felt so at home in the cave that he'd often curl up and go to sleep. The cave loved the feel of the bear's warm soft fur and felt very happy when the bear was there. When the bear left, the pleasant memory of his visit would linger for a long time, and the cave would eagerly await his return.

Then one day the cave heard a thud, and there at his mouth he saw a rock that had fallen from his huge back. The cave was dismayed to see part of himself lying there, and he quickly picked it up and drew it inside. A few days later there was another sound outside, and looking out the cave saw that this time several rocks had fallen from his back and rolled just outside his mouth. Again he rescued them, bringing them inside himself.

Then the day came when the bear returned once again for a visit, and the cave was overjoyed to see him. The bear saw the pile of rocks in his usual resting place, pushed them gently aside and lay down peacefully in his beloved cave. And then he got up and left and went about his work again.

When the bear returned later to the cave, there were considerably more rocks. He didn't like the clutter he saw, but since he loved the cave so much, he stayed and tried to relax with the cave, though it took some doing to push aside the rocks enough to be comfortable.

Each time the bear came after that it seemed to get worse. The cave kept hauling in more and more rocks, desperately trying not to lose a bit of his precious self. There was a big pile of rocks of his desires and plans. Another pile of old hurts and fears that he hugged to himself. Still another rockpile of worries. Oh, ever so many piles of rocks, I couldn't name them all. And so each time the bear came, there was less and less room for him. His visits grew shorter as the crowding increased. Finally he stopped coming altogether.

At first the cave hardly noticed this, so preoccupied was he with each of his rocks. But one day he started thinking of the good old times he'd spent with the bear, and was startled to realize how long it had been since he'd seen him. He couldn't imagine why the bear had stopped coming. He missed him sorely. He waited day after day for the bear, but he never appeared. Then one day he heard familiar footsteps and looked out of his door—there was the bear disappearing around the corner. He called out, but it was too late. The bear was gone.

Some days later he heard those footsteps again. This time he was quicker and caught the bear at his door. "Why don't you come here any more?" asked the cave. "Because there's no room for me here," said the bear. "Look." And the cave looked within and was startled to see that what the bear said was true. His nice inviting hollow was completely filled in with himself. All those rocks that had fallen over the years had been piled inside and clung tightly to, until there was no room for anything else.

When the cave saw what he had done, he wept softly. What could he do? How could he reverse all those years of work? "I'm sorry," he said to the bear. "I want to make room for you. Please help me." "I will," said the bear.

"But it can't be done all at once. Little by little we'll clear them out."

The cave was eager to get on with it. "Take them all, you can have them," he said. But he was told he'd have to hand them over stone by stone. And so he began—turning them over stone by stone for the bear to carry away. It wasn't too long before he met with a strange reluctance. How attached he had become to some of those rocks! They seemed like old friends, and so he delayed in handing some of them over. Yet no matter how attached he was to the rocks, he longed for bear's presence even more. So each time the bear came, he gave him some rocks to carry away. He invited the wind in to help too. The wind howled through him, loosening those rocks that had wedged themselves firmly in place over the years. Then it blew in water to wash him clean.

The whole process took a long time. But finally the day came when the cave was nicely hollowed out again, and neat and clean. The bear lay down and snuggled up in the cave's cozy hollow. How good his soft fur felt, how peaceful and serene his presence. As the cave was enjoying the bear's quiet presence, he heard the sound of a rock falling. He stifled a sudden impulse to pull it inside, and thought instead, "I know what I'll do, I'll give it to the bear; he'll know what to do with it."

*The hungry he has filled with good things,
and the rich sent empty away.* –Luke 1:53

THE BOY, THE CAT,
AND THE BUSH

The Boy

ONCE there was a boy with a sad heart. He was lonely and sad. "I'm no good to anyone," he thought. "No good, no good at all. Look at Sam. Everyone likes Sam. He makes them laugh. I can't make anyone laugh."

People would go by. Sometimes they wouldn't notice boy, because boy was so quiet. Sometimes they would, and say hello. But sometimes boy didn't answer. People would say, "How unfriendly boy is, he never says hello; he probably doesn't like us." But boy did like people. Yet sometimes his sad heart was so heavy he couldn't notice them, even though he wanted to.

One day John came by and said hello. "Hello," answered boy back shyly. And John sat down beside boy. And it felt good.

Then John had to go away. And boy felt lonely. "I wish he would come back," he thought. John did come back; and they spent a lot of time together.

When John left again, boy knew he wasn't alone. For he had a very special place in John's heart. Wherever John went, boy went too—in John's heart. And John had a very special place in boy's heart. Wherever boy went, John went too—in boy's heart. So boy wasn't alone any longer.

The Cat

ONCE there was a cat. A funnier looking cat you never did see. He was black and white. He was furry and shaggy. And he had big feet. He was fierce. At least people thought he was fierce. But he had had a hard life. Once he was caught up in a tree for two days. Once he was caught in a roll of linoleum for three days. And once some mean kids tried to drown him.

So he was afraid of people. People were the enemy. The world was his enemy. He felt alone. Afraid. He felt he had to defend himself. He became very hostile. If anyone came near him, he would fight. He wasn't fighting because he was bad, but because he had to defend himself.

When he wasn't fighting, he would go into a bag or a box and hide from his enemies. If he heard anyone come by, he would stretch out his paw, put out his claws—and scratch! So people avoided him. "Stay away from cat," they said. "Cat is bad. He will hurt you."

One day boy came along and saw cat, and said, "Oh, what a beautiful cat!" He knew cat wasn't bad. He knew cat was good, but had had a hard life. Boy sat beside cat. Cat reached out and scratched him. But boy didn't yell at cat and leave. He stayed and talked gently to cat. "What a strange boy this is," thought cat. He was still afraid, but didn't try to scratch boy again.

Every day boy would come and talk to cat. Cat would stick his head out of the bag and listen. Eventually cat became braver and came out of the bag. Finally one day he went right up to boy and curled up and purred. After that boy and cat spent a lot of time together—lying quietly in the grass and leaping joyfully through the fields.

The Bush

ONCE upon a time there was a beautiful garden. Cat went walking one day through the garden. There were flowers, hundreds of flowers. Flowers of every color. Big flowers and little ones. Blue ones and red ones. There were plants of all kinds. Bushes and trees. Skinny ones and fat ones. Tall ones and short ones. All so lovely.

Yes, all these were in the garden. But in one long-forgotten corner of the garden lived a bush. The skinniest, scraggliest, droopiest bush you ever did see. All the other plants laughed at him. "You don't belong in our garden," they said. "This is a garden for beautiful plants. If only you weren't here, what a lovely garden we'd have."

Bush would try to be brave, and try not to cry. When he couldn't keep the tears back any longer, he'd hide his face and cry and cry and cry. "Why am I so ugly," he wondered. "I wish I were pretty like the others."

Cat walked by all the plants and flowers and trees, looking for the prettiest one of all. Soon he stopped under bush—skinny, scraggly, droopy bush. He smiled at bush, curled up in a ball, and went fast asleep. Bush began to cry. "Why is cat sleeping here?" he thought. "No one ever slept under me before. All the plants laugh at me."

When cat woke up bush asked him, "Why are you sitting under me?" "Because you're beautiful. I like you," said cat. "You're nuts," said bush. Still, bush straightened up a bit.

The next day bush was drooping as much as ever. Cat came by again. "But I'm not beautiful," said bush. "You are," said cat. "You're beautiful because you're you. There's no other like you anywhere. I like you." "You don't like me. Nobody likes me," said bush. But bush wanted to believe someone, someone, could really like him.

Cat came every day. Almost every day anyway. And bush loved to have cat sleep under him. To feel cat's soft warm fur against his feet. To see cat's smile as he said hello and goodbye. "Funny," thought bush. "That cat really seems to like me. But that's ridiculous. No one can like me."

But one day bush found he was perking up and singing a song. And one day, as bush hummed away at his favorite tune, little flowers burst out all over him. "What a beautiful bush," people said. "Why that bush is the loveliest in all the garden. The loveliest bush anywhere."

As I have loved you, so you must love one another.   –John 13:34

PART 2

THE PEBBLE THAT WAS GOOD FOR NOTHING

ONCE there was a little pebble lying on the ground. He had lain there for years with other pebbles. At first it had been quite uncomfortable—some of the other pebbles had been quite abrasive, rubbing against him with their sharp edges. How irritating it had been! But over years of rubbing, they had rounded and smoothed each other off and now they lay content together in silent companionship. Pebble enjoyed lying in the warm sun, looking up at the blue sky, watching clouds go by and birds flying overhead. But he was often trod underfoot, and he hated being walked on. He hated being small and weak and insignificant and good for nothing.

He wished he were good for something. The stream at his side supplied water to the thirsty, and was the home of many kinds of fish. The tree next to it gave shelter to birds and provided shade from the heat of hot summer days. The clouds above brought rain to the earth, making gardens grow.

But he was good for nothing and could do none of these things. That rock nearby was often used as a seat upon which the weary could rest from their journeys. Once when he was young he thought he would grow up to be a big strong rock like that, providing a resting place for travelers. Or better yet, he hoped he might grow up to become the cornerstone of a magnificent building. Or maybe he'd become a mighty boulder sitting high above the countryside, enjoying the splendid view. But he never grew at all. He watched the grass grow, the tree grow, the birds grow—but all the time he remained just a tiny weak little pebble, trodden underfoot, unnoticed and useless.

One day a shepherd boy walked by. Pebble saw the foot coming down and braced himself for the blow. But the boy glanced down, and for some reason his eye was attracted by pebble. Maybe it was his smooth satin finish that caught the boy's eye. Or the sun sparkling on his warm reddish color. Whatever it was, the boy bent down and picked pebble up. Pebble enjoyed the caress of the boy's hand, and the boy liked the feel of pebble rolling between his fingers.

After awhile the boy put pebble in his shepherd's bag where pebble took a nice long rest. Eventually the boy took him out again, admired his lovely color and fine finish, and played with him awhile. Sometimes the boy would make music on his harp, and pebble enjoyed listening to the beautiful sounds. It relaxed him and made him feel one with his surroundings. Pebble loved his new companion.

Then one day there came bad news. A mighty army had gathered in the area, threatening the once peaceful countryside. They were ready to kill, take people away as slaves, plunder houses, destroy villages, burn fields. Pebble was terribly worried about his friend. He wished there were something he could do to help. But what could a little pebble do? Nothing. For he was so little and weak, good for nothing.

At the head of the army was a giant of a man, taller than anyone either the shepherd boy or pebble had ever seen. He was dressed in strong armor with a helmet of bronze upon his head. He carried the sharpest sword and spear to be found anywhere. He challenged anyone to fight him, but no one dared to. Everyone was terrified. Who

84

could possibly be victorious over such a man. There was no one nearly as big and strong as he. To take him on would surely mean death. The people whispered among themselves and tried to come up with a solution, all to no avail.

Finally David—that was the shepherd's name—did a very foolish and rather crazy thing. He came forward and volunteered to fight the giant soldier. Everyone tried to dissuade him. "How could you fight him," they said. "He's gigantic, you're small. He's dressed in fine armor and has the best weapons available, but you have none. He's been a soldier all his life, you're just a boy with no experience."

But David insisted and started toward the giant. The giant in turn approached the shepherd boy. As the giant came closer he was filled with scorn, for here was just a nice good-looking inexperienced boy. What harm could he do?

Pebble was horrified as the massive soldier drew closer. His heart pounded. What chance did his little friend have. How could he escape this heavily armed giant bearing down on him. How pebble wished he could do something to help, to save the shepherd boy. But he was such a tiny thing, powerless and good for nothing.

Suddenly the boy ran toward the giant, and pebble was startled to feel the boy put his hand into his bag, pick him up and take him out. David said a little prayer, put pebble in his sling, swung him round and round above his head, then let him go. Whiz! Pebble flew swiftly through the air, directly towards the immense warrior. He hit the giant on the forehead, broke his skull, and the menacing soldier toppled forward to the ground. When they saw that their leader was dead, the rest of the enemy army turned and fled in terror. The people were free!

So it was that David defeated the giant with pebble! Everyone was astounded. Pebble was absolutely amazed. He had felt so useless, too little to do anything. But in the boy's hand he had slain the evil giant and won a great victory! As he lay there in astonishment, he heard familiar footsteps. It was David approaching. He leaned over, picked pebble up, and put him back in his bag. Pebble was grateful that the boy and his people had been freed from danger. Grateful that he had had a part in it. Now he knew it didn't matter that he was little and small and powerless. For he *was* good for something. All he needed to do was stay near the boy, be ready, and let the boy do with him whatever he will.

When I am weak, then I am strong.
−2 Cor. 12:10

A Christmas Fable
THE BRUISED REED

ONCE there was a reed, tall and proud, growing near a stream. He was a fine reed indeed, and how he loved life! He lived every moment to the full. From his height he had a splendid view of the whole area. He watched the small animals scampering to and fro, the birds darting here and there, the multi-hued insects, the fish gliding in the stream. But best of all he liked the flowers. They came in a never-ending parade of exquisite form and color. Old friends would go, but new ones promptly followed and delighted him so, that he never stopped to wonder what happened to the old. And all the while he stood tall and green. Yes, life was good indeed.

Then one morning he awoke, and as he looked into the stream he discovered that his tip was turning brown. His dismay grew as day after day the malady spread, until his fine green coat was completely gone. Not only that, he began to feel dry, then drier and drier. Then the rains came and beat at him, the wind battered him, and finally a mighty gust snapped him loose from the earth. He lay desolate on the ground, broken, bruised, and heavy-hearted.

Some days later a young man came by and picked him up. He put him in his bag where it was black, so black that poor reed could see nothing at all. He longed for the end, for anything but this unending darkness.

Finally the day came when the young man took him back out of the bag. How good to see light again! And he saw fields and rolling hills and sheep grazing peacefully around. The young man took a sharp knife and cut part of reed away, hurting him so acutely he couldn't help but cry out. Then the man ruthlessly pierced him through from end to end, clearing out his hollow. Every inch of his being quivered with pain. Then he was thrust back into the darkness again.

Sometime later he was taken out again. He welcomed the light, yet dreaded the pain he anticipated would come along with it. And sure enough, there was the knife. This time the young man mercilessly cut several holes in him. He wept silently. Then he was plunged once more into blackness.

The day came when reed from his dark home in the bag sensed something different about him, some excitement in the air. The young man joined some other shepherds and they hurried toward the edge of town. There they went into a cave, and the young man pulled reed out of the bag. Reed braced himself for the inevitable knife. Instead to this surprise, he felt only the gentle caress of the young man's hands as he lifted him tenderly to his lips. Then the young man poured his life breath into him, and there came forth from reed a beautiful song, simple and pure. And as reed sang he looked out and saw a young mother and her little baby. And they smiled at him.

---

*The people that walked in darkness has
seen a great light.*   —Isaiah 9:1

THE BOY WHO HAD
NOTHING TO GIVE

ONCE there was a young boy who loved to look at the birds of the air, the flowers of the fields, the clear blue lakes. These delighted him, and so he spent most of his free time outside, wandering around the countryside. One day he saw a crowd gather. He drew closer to see why. They were listening to a man. There was something about that man that attracted the boy. He sat down and listened too. He was spellbound by what he heard. Never had he heard anyone who spoke to his heart so.

From then on he kept his eye out for the man. Whenever the man was in his area, he quickly knew of it, and avidly listened to everything he had to say. He grew to love the man more and more. He envied the man's disciples, those men who travelled with him wherever he went. He couldn't wait until he grew up and could do the same.

In his gratitude for all the man gave to him through his presence, his words, and the great compassion and love in his eyes, he longed to give the man something in return. But he had nothing to give.

One day he met the man's mother. She had come out to where he was talking to give him a message. The boy followed her home and asked her to tell him more about the man. She told him how shortly after he was born some wise men had come from far away and presented him with gifts of gold, frankincense and myrrh. And about the little shepherd boy who had given him a lamb. And the boy remembered how he himself had once seen a pretty lady pour sweet smelling perfume over the man's feet. How he wished he had such gifts to give!

Often after that the boy returned to the house of the man's mother. He felt at home there and spent many lovely hours learning about the man from her. One day as he left her house to see if the man was in the area, she gave him a few small loaves of bread she had just taken out of the oven. And as he walked along he stopped at the side of a lake and fished awhile. Then he continued on his way with the few loaves and the two fish he had caught. Finally he caught sight of a crowd. And yes, there the man was, talking to their hearts.

The man had much to say that day, and the people listened, fascinated. It grew later and later, and the boy sensed the people around him were getting hungry. He was glad he had brought the bread and fish with him. He could share it with that tired old man at his side, and that mother with her little child to carry. But what of all the others? There were so many of them, and they hadn't anticipated they'd be in this lonely place for so long. There was no place nearby where they could buy food, and it was a long way back to the village. The boy's heart went out to them, but he was just a young boy and there was nothing he could do.

Then one of the man's disciples came up to him. He said the man had asked for the boy's bread and fish. The boy was happy to give them to the man, but at the same time he felt bad that now there was nothing for that tired old man beside him and that mother with her little child to carry. How he wished he had more to give.

Then he saw the man take his loaves and fish and bless them and give thanks over them. And then he started giving them to the people nearest him. Then to those a little further on. And so he went through the crowd, giving each person some bread and fish. Then he came to the mother carrying her child and to that tired old man near the boy. And there was enough for them. Finally he stopped right in front of the boy and gave him some bread and fish too. The boy's heart stopped—never had he been so close to the man before. As he looked into the man's eyes, he understood that he didn't need a lot to give. It was so simple really. All he had to do was give the little bit he had, and the man would do the rest.

My son, give me your heart.
–Prov. 23:26

THE ELEVENTH HOUR

MY name is Nathan. I am a day laborer. I want to tell you about the day I met Jesus of Nazareth. It was the time of the grape harvest. The vineyard owners were anxious to get their grapes in before the rains came and ruined the crop. I got up before dawn so I'd be there at the marketplace when the first vineyard owner arrived. But most of the other laborers did the same, and there were more of us waiting to be hired than were needed.

We were desperate for work. The lot of a servant was much better. They had steady work, food, shelter. Even the slaves had the security of a roof over their heads and a bite to eat every day. But we were dependent day by day upon someone hiring us. If they did, our wives and children had something to eat. If not, they'd often go to bed hungry. Well, I didn't want my beloved Rachel and my little Reuben and Aaron to suffer, so I was there when the first vineyard owner came along. He picked a dozen men and left. I was not among them.

Other vineyard owners came. I'd rush forward, but never seemed quick enough, so fierce was the competition for work. The day dragged on, and those of us still waiting chatted and tried to cheer each other on. My friend Levi was especially despondent over not being hired. He had an infant son who was quite ill. It seemed his only hope was in a rare medicinal herb which he could purchase with his day's earnings—he didn't mind going hungry himself to

save the child. But now the day was quickly passing, and his hope was fading with it.

Finally in mid-afternoon a vineyard owner returned, looking for more workers. I could have gone this time. But I felt sorry for my friend Levi and pushed him forward instead. And now there wasn't much chance left for me.

I worried about my family. I'd much rather be sweating in the fields than standing here waiting, worrying about them. Perhaps I could glean a few grains from an empty field on the way home or find a few berries to tide my family over to the next day. I waited awhile longer. Then, just as I was about to leave, one of the landowners came back. To my surprise he came right up to me and asked me why I was standing there idle. I told him it was because no one had hired me. He told me to come. There was no talk of pay. At that point I would have been happy to work the rest of the day for a crust of bread, any little bit was better than going home empty handed.

The end of the day came quickly and we lined up to receive our pay. I was called up first, I who had started work at the eleventh hour. I can't tell you my surprise when the master handed me a full day's pay! I thought it must be a mistake and started to explain, but he waved me on. I saw my friend Levi go up and he got a full day's pay too. He was so happy that now, unexpectedly, he could get that medicine for his son. Those who came at the third hour received the same. Finally those who had worked the full day came up, and they too received one day's pay.

Well, they didn't like that too much. Some were quite outraged. "We worked hard and sweated all day," they grumbled, "and you give us the same as those who worked only an hour. That's not fair." The master replied to one of these, "Friend, I'm not being unfair to you. Didn't you agree to work for the usual wage? Take your pay and go.

I want to give the man I hired last the same as you. Don't I have the right to do as I want with my own money? Or are you jealous because I am generous?" The man walked away.

Levi and I were quite taken aback by our unexpected good fortune. We walked away in silence, our hearts full of wonder and joy. We passed a man who had been watching all that had happened. He looked at us with love and said, "The kingdom of heaven is like that." These words made a deep impression upon me. I wanted to know more about this kingdom. Not long after I sought this man, Jesus of Nazareth, and became a follower of his. I've been learning more about the kingdom of heaven ever since.

The last shall be first, and the first shall be last.   Matthew 20:16

ARTEMIUS'S TESTIMONY

MY name is Artemius. I want to tell you about the day my life was changed. I was a seller of pigeons and doves in the temple. I'd done it for years. When I was young I had a great love for the Lord and for the temple. I wanted to be close to it. I wanted to have some part in making oblations available to the Lord. So I decided to be a pigeon seller.

At first it was just what I wanted. I was close to the temple, and would often stop my work for times of quiet prayer with my God. But some of the others laughed at me. I wouldn't get anywhere that way they said. I'd miss a sale, I'd have things stolen leaving them unattended. They were well dressed. They bragged about the things they bought their wives and children. About the better education they could provide for them.

I wanted these good things for my family too. So gradually I stopped taking time out for prayer and spent more and more time at my business. I raised my prices and started talking my customers into paying more, buying a more expensive bird than they had originally intended. A more worthy offering for the Lord, I glibly told them. It should hurt a little if the Lord were to heed their prayers.

One day was especially busy—never in a single day had I raked in so much money! Such a record! I was gloating over it, thinking of the party we'd throw to impress our friends, of the stunning new dress my wife would wear, of the wine we'd serve, the finest available. Then a man came in. He saw the buying and selling. I tell you, I'd never

99

seen it at such a feverish pitch as it was that day—the sellers exhorting people to pay a little more for a more pleasing offering, people who could barely afford a decent meal for their family.

This man, well, he turned to us, whip in hand, and with a voice full of authority such as I had never heard before, he proclaimed the temple a house of prayer and said we were making it a den of thieves. In his anger he drove many of us out and overturned tables. Mine was one of them. One woman rushed back and picked up the money I had just robbed her of. Only then did I notice how worn and tired and worried she looked, and hungry too.

In the face of this man's anger, I could not leave like some did. I could not yell back and ask what right he had to do this. For as I looked at him something touched me at the core of my being. And I knew right then and there that my life would never be the same. I was convicted and knew in my heart I had been acting wrongly. I turned to my God and said I was sorry. And immediately there sprang forth once again that old desire for prayer, for God. I picked up the money and distributed it to the beggars around the temple. I gave away the few birds left and went home.

I didn't know what to say to my wife. She was expecting a good take as there were so many people come from out of town for the festival, and here I was with nothing. But before I could say anything, she started telling me about the man she had heard preaching that day. She was so moved she had invited him and his followers in for dinner. It turned out he was the same man I had encountered in the temple. I didn't need to tell her anything. She understood. We got rid of some of the extra things around the house and started to live more simply. I took a holiday from the business and spent some time in prayer and fasting, wondering what to do with my life. In the end I went back to the business. But honestly this time. And I took time out to pray, and to talk to people, sharing their sorrows and joys. When I saw someone who couldn't afford an offering, I made sure they got one anyway. We didn't suffer. We had all we needed. And since we lived more simply than before we had enough to give away.

And the kids—they took it well, they did. I wasn't always buying things for them like before, but they didn't seem to mind. We spent more time together, and I guess that's what mattered to them. My, what fine kids I have!

My oldest son Elias, now, he was a bit of a problem, I'll admit. He resented our new way of living at first. Guess I spoiled him pretty badly giving him everything he ever wanted. So after my experience with this man—Jesus was his name—Elias expected things to be like they had always been. "Papa, get me this, Papa, get me that," he'd say. And though I'd try to explain, he never understood, and would sulk and pout for days. I knew he resented this man Jesus, and I didn't know what to do. But every day in the temple I just used to thank God for Elias and offer him back to God. And you know what? One day Elias met Jesus himself. And he hasn't been the same since! He's offered to help me with the business. And what a help he is. Now I can leave anytime to pray and my boy will carry on. And the people, he's so good with them, such a listener, everyone loves him. Why, business is better than ever. He gives birds away too, more than I ever did. But he has a way about him, he does, giving people odd jobs to do to pay for them, seems they feel better about it then. That's my son Elias, what a fine boy!

This man Jesus travels around a lot. We don't see too much of him. But when he's in our area, sometimes he and his friends have supper at our house. It's such a special occasion. We treasure his answers to our questions.

Well, that's my story. And believe me, I'll never forget the day this man came roaring through the temple with a whip in his hand. For that was the day my life was changed.

My house will be called a house of prayer for all the peoples.   –Isaiah 56:7

An Easter Story
THE OLD MAN WITH NEW EYES

ONCE there was an old man. He was very unhappy
and didn't enjoy life very much. As things were
never right, he grumbled and complained. He grumbled
that he had to get up in the morning, then when nightfall
came, it came too soon. He complained when he had to
work, and found it boring when he didn't. He murmured
that people didn't pay enough attention to him, and when
they did, it annoyed or irritated him. He hated it when it
rained and found the sun too hot when it came out. In
winter he longed for summer and in summer for fall. All
in all, life was rather miserable.

One day he stopped at a fruit stand. He found some of
the fruit was too ripe, and the rest not ripe enough. And so
he left again. As he was leaving, the fruit seller said to
him, "I wish you new eyes, sir, child eyes." "New eyes,"
thought the old man as he walked away. "Why, my
eyesight is perfect. I've never needed glasses in my life,
and my vision is sharper than that of many folks half my
age. I see things every bit as clearly as I did as a child."

A week or so later he stopped at the fruit stand again.
The fruit seller had the fruit he didn't want, and the fruit
he wanted wasn't there. As he was leaving the fruit seller
said "I wish you kingdom eyes, sir." "Kingdom eyes?"
This puzzled the old man a bit. But no matter. He was a
busy man, lots of things to do, and so he let it pass.

Sometime later the old man stopped at the fruit stand again. Same old story. Everything he didn't want, nothing he did want, everything too ripe or not ripe enough. And as he left, the fruit seller said, "I wish you treasure-hunting eyes, sir." "Treasure-hunting eyes?" Why he had been on a treasure-hunt once. And of all in the group, it had been he who had finally spotted the treasure. Why if anyone had treasure-hunting eyes, he had. But where had it gotten him? There had been endless squabbling over the treasure, and in the end he had never received his share. Treasure-hunting eyes indeed!

But in spite of himself the old man began to wonder about what the fruit seller had said to him. What did he mean, new eyes, child eyes, kingdom eyes, treasure-hunting eyes? The next time he stopped at the stand, he pressed the fruit seller to explain.

"Well, you see," the fruit seller began, "one day there was a stranger in town. Quite a crowd gathered to hear him speak. I joined them. He spoke of many things, but a few things he said really stuck in my mind. He said the kingdom of heaven was within you, was like a treasure hidden in a field, and that unless you become like a little child you could not enter it. I did not understand what he meant, but I wondered on it, and carried his words in my heart.

"The next day the stranger was there again. And there was a blind man there, a man blind from birth, I believe. He went up to the stranger and said to him, 'Sir, if you want to, you can make me see.' And the stranger answered, 'Of course I want to,' and would you believe, the blind man's eyes were opened and he could see, he really could. And how he delighted in all he saw. And it seemed to me then that I did not see rightly. For though I saw, I was not happy with what I saw the way this blind man was. And so, without hardly thinking about it, I blurted out to the stranger, 'Please sir, give me new eyes.' 'I will,' he answered, 'I give you child eyes, kingdom eyes, treasure-hunting eyes.' I thanked him and left.

"That was the last time I ever saw the stranger. But from that time on I saw things differently. Where before I saw only darkness, I saw stars and fireflies. Where before I found only pain, I discovered a door to joy. Where before I had seen nothing worthwhile, I found much to marvel at. Where before I lived in a desert of doubt and despair, a fountain of faith and hope sprung up. And where before people annoyed or irritated or bored me, I saw something in them that reminded me of the stranger. And I rejoiced."

The old man went away wondering at what the fruit seller had told him. He shrugged it off at first, but no matter how he tried to ignore it, the story kept coming back to mind. And the more he thought about it, the more he began to long for new eyes for himself. He began to think about the stranger, to hope he would return. And when he did, he would ask for new eyes too.

The thought excited him. But he began to worry that when he saw the stranger he would be too nervous to ask for anything. And so he figured he would practice what to say. "Give me new eyes, sir, child eyes, kingdom eyes, treasure-hunting eyes." Yes, that is what he would say. Day and night he practiced this, to be sure he'd never forget, no matter how shaky he was when he saw the stranger.

And after awhile he put it to music, made it into a little song:

Give me new eyes, sir, child eyes, king-dom eyes, trea-sure hun-ting eyes. Give me new eyes ____ .

Yes, that was the refrain he sang many times a day, day after day, month after month. He kept alert for news of the stranger, but none came. Over a year went by. But the old man kept hoping and singing his song.

Then one day when he stopped at the fruit stand, he found the fruit seller very sad indeed. "What's the matter?" he asked. "I've just received news," said the fruit seller, "that the stranger who gave me new eyes has been arrested, and is being put to death this very day."

The old man went home and cried and cried. His chance was gone. Now he would never meet the stranger. Now he would never have new eyes.

Yet the song had become so much a part of him that he continued to sing it. And as he was singing the song on the third day after hearing the tragic news of the stranger, he suddenly felt something like scales fall from his eyes. And he began to see things differently.

Where before he saw only darkness, he saw stars and fireflies. Where before he saw only the injuries done him and resented them, he saw how much he was loved and found a forgiveness that healed his wounds. Where before he had seen nothing of value, he found hidden many treasures. Where before he had passed his days in boredom and suspicion, he now lived in wonderment and trust. And where before people had irritated him, he saw something in them that made him think of the stranger. And he knew that the stranger lived.

After shadow and darkness, the eyes of the blind will see.   –Isaiah 29:18

PART 3

THE SHUT-UP POSY

ONCE there was a posy. It wasn't a common kind of posy that blows out wide open so everybody can see its outside and its inside too. It was one of those posies that don't come till way towards fall. They're sort of blue, but real dark, and they look as if they were buds instead of posies—only buds open out, and these don't. They're all shut up, closed tight, and never, never open. It doesn't matter how much sun they get, how much rain, whether it's cold or hot, those posies stay shut up tight. But if you pick them open very carefully with a pin, you find they're real pretty inside. You couldn't find a posy that was finished off better, soft and nice, with pretty little stripes painted on them, and all the little things like threads in the middle, such as the open posies have, standing up, with little knots on their tops, oh, so pretty! It makes you think hard. What are they that way for? If they aren't going to open out, what's the use of having the shut-up part so slicked up and nice, with nobody ever seeing it? Some folks call them closed gentians, but I always call them the shut-up posies.

Well, it's one of that kind of posy that I'm going to tell you about. She was one of the most shut-up of them all, all blacky-blue, and straight up and down, shut-up fast and tight. Nobody would ever dream she was pretty inside. And the funniest thing is, she didn't know it herself! At first she thought she was a bud, like lots of buds all around her, and she counted on opening like they did. But when the days kept passing by, and all the other buds opened out, and showed how pretty they were, and she didn't open, why then she got terribly discouraged.

So then she figured she was a mistake somehow, that she should have been a posy, and was begun for one, but wasn't finished, and she was awfully unhappy. She knew there were pretty posies all around, golden rod and daisies and lots of others. And their inside was the right side, and they were proud of it, and held it open, and showed the pretty lining, all soft and nice with the little fuzzy yellow threads standing up with little balls on their tips. And the shut-up posy felt real bad. Not mean and hateful and begrudging, you know, and wanting to take away the nice part from the other posies, but sorry and kind of ashamed.

"Oh, dear me!" she said, "What a homely, skimpy, awkward thing I am! I'm not more than half made. There's no nice pretty lining inside of me, like in those other posies. And only my wrong side shows, and that's just plain and common. I can't cheer up folks like the goldenrod and daisies do. Nobody wants to pick me and carry me home. I'm no good to anybody and never will be." So she kept on thinking these dreadfully sorry thoughts, and mostly wishing she'd never been made at all.

She'd see the dew lying soft and cool on the other posies' faces, and the sun shining warm on them as they held them up, and sometimes she'd see a butterfly come down and light on them real soft, and kind of put his head down to them as if he were kissing them, and she thought it would be wonderfully nice to hold her face up to all those pleasant things. But she couldn't.

Then one day, before she got very old, before she dried up or fell off or anything like that, she saw somebody coming along. It was a man and he was looking at all the posies real hard, but he wasn't picking any of them. Seems as if he was looking for something different from what he

saw, and the poor little shut-up posy began to wonder what he was after. Timidly she asked him in her shut-up whispering voice. And the man said, "I'm picking posies. That's what I work at most of the time. It's not for myself, but the one I work for. I'm only his help. I run errands and do chores for him, and it's a particular kind of posy he's sent me for today." "What does he want them for?" said the shut-up posy. "Why, to plant in his garden," said the man. "He's got the most beautiful garden you ever saw, and I pick posies for it." "Dear me," thought the shut-up posy, "I wish he'd pick me. But I'm not the kind, I know." Then she said, so softly he could hardly hear her, "What sort of posies are you after this time?" "Well," said the man, "it's a difficult order I have today. I've got to find a posy that's handsomer inside than it is outside, one that folks haven't noticed here because it's homely and queer to look at, never knowing that inside it's as handsome as any posy on earth. Seen any of that kind?"

Well, the poor shut-up posy was terribly worked up. She thought, "Oh dear! If only they'd finished me off inside! I'm the right kind outside, homely and queer enough, but there's nothing worth looking at inside, I'm sure of that." But she didn't say this or anything else out loud, and by and by, when the man had waited and didn't get any answer, he began to look at the shut-up posy more closely, to see why she was so mum. Then suddenly he said, "Looks to me as if you might be that kind yourself, are you?" "Oh no, no, no!" whispered the shut-up posy. "I wish I was, I wish I was. I'm all right outside, homely and awkward and queer as can be, but I'm not pretty inside, I know I'm not." "I'm not so sure of that myself," said the man, "but I can tell in a jiffy." "Will you have to pick me to pieces?" said the shut-up posy. "No," said the man. "I've got a way of telling. The one I work for showed me." The shut-up posy never knew what he did to her, but it was something soft and pleasant, and it didn't hurt a bit. Then the man said, "Well, well, well!" That's all he said, but he took her up real gently, and began to carry her away. "Where are you taking me?" asked the shut-up posy. "Where you belong," said the man, "to the garden of the one I work for." "I didn't know I was nice enough inside," said the shut-up posy, very soft and still. "They most generally don't," said the man.

He chose the lowly things of this world and the despised things. –1 Cor. 1:27-28

THE HORSE THAT
BELIEVED HE'D GET THERE

ONCE there was a nice horse named Jack who worked on a threshing machine. The old treadmill kind where the horses keep stepping up on a board thing as if they were climbing up hill or going up a pair of stairs, only they don't ever move along a bit. They keep right in the same place all the time, stepping and stepping, but never moving on.

The first time they put Jack on to thresh, he didn't know what the machine was, and he walked along and up the boards quickly and lively, and he didn't see why he didn't get along any faster. There was a horse beside him named Billy, a kind of fretting, cross fellow, and he saw through it right away.

"Don't go along," he said to Jack. "It's no use. You won't ever get anywhere, they're fooling us, and I won't give in to them." So Billy hung back and shook his head and tried to get away and kick, and the man whipped him and hollered at them. But Jack, he went on quietly and quickly and pleasantly, stepping away, and he said softly to Billy, "Come along, it's all right, we'll be there by and by. Don't you see, I'm getting along already?" And that was the way things went everyday.

Jack never gave up. He climbed and climbed, walked and walked, just as if he saw the place he was going to, and as if it was getting nearer and nearer. And every night when they took him off, he was as pleased with his day's

journey as if he'd gone twenty miles. "I've done first-rate today," he'd say to cross, kicking Billy. "The roads were good, and I never picked up a stone or dropped a shoe, and I got along a good piece. I'll be there pretty soon." "Why," said Billy, "what a foolish fellow you are! You've been in the same spot all day, and haven't got along one bit. And what do you mean by 'there'? Where is it you think you're going anyway?"

"Well, I don't exactly know," said Jack, "but I'm getting there real well. I almost saw it once today." He didn't mind Billy's laughing at him, and trying to keep him from being satisfied. He just went on trying and trying to get there, and hoping and believing he would after a while. He was always spry and comfortable, took his work real easy, relished his food and drink, and slept first rate nights. But Billy fretted and scolded and kicked and bit, and that made him hot and tired, and got him whipped and hollered at, and pulled and yanked. He didn't have anything in his mind to cheer him up, for he didn't believe anything good was coming as Jack did. He always knew it wasn't, but Jack always knew it was. And Jack took notice of things that Billy never saw at all. He saw the trees growing and heard the birds singing, and the brook gurgling along over the stones, and he watched the butterflies flying, and sometimes a big yellow one would land right on his back. Jack took notice of them all, and he'd say, "I'm getting along now for sure, for there are birds and flowers and flying things here I never saw a ways back. I guess I'm almost there!" "There, there!", Billy would say. "Where is it, anyway? I've never seen any of those flowers and creatures you talk about, and I'm right beside you on these old boards the whole time."

All the children around there liked Jack. They'd watch the two horses working, and they saw Billy all cross and skittish, holding back and shaking his head and trying to kick, never taking any notice of them or anything. And they saw Jack stepping along lively and spry, pleasant and willing, turning his head when they came up to him, and looking friendly at them out of his kind brown eyes. And the boys and girls would say, "Good Jack! Nice old Jack!" And they'd pat him, and give him an apple, or a carrot, or something good. But they didn't give Billy any. They didn't like his ways, and they were afraid he'd bite their fingers. And come evening Jack would say, "It's getting nicer and nicer as we get further on the road, isn't it? Folks are pleasanter, and the food is better, and things are more comfortable in every way, and I figure by that that we're almost there." But Billy would grumble, "It's worse and worse, young ones bothering the life out of me, the birds jabbering and the flowers smelling until my head aches. O dear me, I'm almost dead." And so it went.

Jack had every bit as much hard work to do as Billy, but he didn't mind, he was so full of what was coming, and how good it would be to get there. And because he was pleasant and willing and worked so well, and because he took notice of all the nice things around him and saw new ones every day, he was treated real kind and never got tired and worn out and low in spirits like Billy. Even the flies didn't pester him like they did Billy, for when he felt them biting and crawling he figured the summer was almost over and they'd be there in a jiffy now.

I don't know the rest of this story, or what 'there' was, but I believe Jack got there. Maybe it was just dying peacefully and quietly, and resting after all that stepping and climbing. He'd have liked that, especially when he knew folks were sorry to have him go and would always remember him. Maybe it was just living on and on, interested and enjoying, and liked by folks, and then being taken away from the hard work and put out to pasture for the rest of his days. It might have been a lot of things, but I feel pretty sure he got it, and that he was glad he hadn't given up believing it would come. For you remember, all the time when Billy most knew it wasn't coming, Jack most knew it was.

We can be full of joy here and now, even in our trials and troubles. These very things will give us patient endurance; this in turn will develop a mature character; and a character of this sort produces a steady hope, a hope that will never disappoint us.   –Romans 5:3-4

THE PLANT THAT
LOST ITS BERRY

ONCE there was a plant, and it had just one little
berry. And the berry was real pretty to look at. The
plant set everything on her little berry. She thought there
never was in all the world such a beautiful berry as hers,
so prettily shaped and so whitish blue, with such a soft skin
and pink stem, and especially with that nice white striped
stone inside of it. She held it all day and all night tight and
fast. When it rained real hard, and the wind blew, she kind
of stretched out some of her leaves and covered her little
berry up, and she did the same when the sun was too hot.
And the berry grew and grew, and was so fat and smooth
and pretty! And the plant was just wrapped up in her little
berry, loving it terribly hard, and being dreadfully proud
of it too.

Well, one day, all of a sudden, when the plant wasn't
thinking of a storm coming, a little wind rose up. It wasn't
a gale, it wasn't half as hard as the berry had seen lots of
times and never got hurt or anything. And the plant wasn't
expecting any danger, when all of a sudden there came a
little bit of a snap, and the slim little pink stem broke, and
the little berry fell and rolled away, and before you knew
it, it was clear out of sight. I can't begin to tell you how
the plant carried on. Seemed as if she'd die or go raving
crazy. It's only folks who've lost just what they treasure
most who can understand it. She wouldn't believe it at
first. She thought she'd wake up and feel her little berry

holding her close, hanging on her, snuggling up to her under the shady leaves.

The other plants tried to cheer her up and help her. One of them told her how it had lost all its little berries itself, a long time back, and how it had somehow stood it and got over it. "But they weren't like mine," thought the poor plant. "There never was a berry like mine, with its pretty figure, its pink slim little neck, and its soft smooth skin." And another plant told her maybe her berry was saved from growing up a trouble to her, getting bad and hard, with maybe a worm inside it to make her ashamed and sorry. "Oh, no, no!" thought the mother plant. "My berry would never have got bad and hard, and I'd have kept any worm from touching its little white heart." Not a single thing the plant folks said to her did a bit of good. Their talk only worried her and pestered her, when she just wanted to be left alone so she could think about her little berry all to herself.

Just where the berry used to hang and where the little pink stem broke off, there was a sore place that ached and smarted all day and all night, and never healed up. And by and by the poor plant got all worn out with the aching and the mourning and the missing, and she felt her heart all drying up and stopping, and her leaves turned yellow and wrinkled, and—she was dead. She couldn't live on without her little berry.

Folks called it being dead, and it looked like it, for there she lay without a sign of life for a long, long spell. It was for days and weeks and months anyway. But it didn't seem so long to the mother plant. She shut her eyes, feeling terribly tired and lonesome, and the next thing she knew she opened them again, and she was wide awake. She hardly knew herself though, she was so fresh and juicy and alive, so kind of young in every way. At first she didn't think of anything but how good and well she felt, and how beautiful things were all around her. Then suddenly she remembered her little berry, and she said to herself, "O dear, dear me! If only my own little berry was here to see me now, and know how I feel!" She thought she said it to herself, but maybe she spoke out loud, for just as she said it somebody answered her. It was an angel, and he said, "Why your little berry does see you. Look there." And she looked, and she saw he was pointing to the most beautiful little plant you ever saw, straight and nice, with little bits of soft green leaves with the sun shining through them, and somehow she knew for sure that it was her little berry.

The angel began to speak. He was going to explain how, if she hadn't lost her berry, it would never have grown into this pretty plant, but he saw all of a sudden that he needn't take the trouble. She showed in her face that she knew all about it, every blessed thing. Even angels aren't much use explaining when it has to do with mothers and their own children. Yes, the mother plant saw it all without any explaining. She was just a bit ashamed, but she was terribly pleased.

Blessed are those who mourn, for they shall be comforted.   –Matthew 5:5

123

THE STONY HEAD

ONCE there was something way up on the side of a mountain that looked like a man's head. The rocks up there had got fixed so they made a great big head and face, and everybody could see it as plain as could be. Folks called it the Stony Head, and they came to see it from miles away. There was a man who lived around there, just where he could see the head from his window. He was a man who things had gone wrong for all along. He'd had lots of trouble, and he didn't take it very easy. He fretted and complained, and blamed it on other folks, and especially on God. And one day when he'd just come to live in those parts, he looked out of his window and saw that Stony Head standing out plain against the sky. It looked real harsh and hard and stony and dark, and all of a sudden the man thought it looked like God.

"Yes," he said to himself, "that's just the way I always knew he looked, harsh and hard and stony and dark, that's him." The man was dreadfully afraid of it, but somehow he couldn't stop looking at it. And by and by he shut himself up there all alone, and spent his whole time just looking at that hard, stony face, and thinking who it was, and who'd brought all his trouble on him. There were poor folks all around that district, but he never did anything to help them. He let them be hungry or thirsty or ailing or shut up in jail or whatever. He never helped them or did anything for them, because he was looking at that head every single minute, and seeing how stony and hard it was, and being scared of it and the one he thought it looked like.

Folks who were in trouble came along and knocked at his door, but he never opened it a bit, even to see who was there. Sheep and lambs that were lost came straying into his yard, but he never took them in or showed them the way home. He wasn't any good to anyone, not even to himself, for he was terribly unhappy and scared and angry. So it went on for years and years, and the man was still there shut up all alone, looking and looking and scared at looking at that harsh, hard, stony face and head. But one day as he was sitting there by the window looking, he heard a little sound. I don't know what made him hear it just then. There had been such sounds as that time and time again, and he never took any notice. It was like a child crying, and that's common enough.

But this time it seemed different, and he couldn't help taking notice. He tried not to hear it, but he had to. It was a little child crying as if it had lost its way and was scared, and the man found he couldn't stand it somehow. Maybe the reason was that he'd once had a little boy of his own, and lost him. That was one of the things he blamed on God, and thought about when he looked at the Stone Head. Anyway, he couldn't stand the crying this time, and he got up, and before he knew it he'd opened the door and gone out. He hadn't been out in the sunshine and fresh air for a long spell, and it made him dizzy at first. But he heard the crying again, and he ran to find the child. But he couldn't find it. Every time he thought he was close to it, he'd hear the crying a little further off. And he'd go on and on, stumbling over stones and falling over logs and stepping into holes. But he stuck to it, forgetting everything but the little crying voice ahead of him. It seemed he just must find that little lost child, as if he'd be more than willing to give up his own poor lonesome old life to save him. And just as he came to thinking that, he saw something moving ahead of him, and he knew he'd found the lost child.

Before he thought what he was doing, he got down on his knees just like he used to before he got angry at God, and he was going to thank him for helping him to save that child. But then he remembered. It came back to him who God was, and how he had seen his head, with the harsh stony face up on the mountain, and that made him look at it again. And oh! What do you think he saw? There was the same head up there, no mistake about that, but the face, oh, the face was so different! It wasn't harsh or hard or dark any more. There was such a loving, beautiful, kind sort of look on it now. Somehow it made the man think a bit of the way his father who had died ever so long ago, used to look at him when he was a boy and had been bad and then was sorry and ashamed. Oh, it was the most beautiful face you ever saw! "Oh, what does it mean?" said the man. "What's changed the face so? What in the world's made it so different?"

And just then an angel came up close to him. It was a little young angel, and maybe it was what he'd taken for a lost child and what he'd been following for so far. And the angel said, "The face hasn't changed a bit. It was just like that all the time, only you're looking at it from a different point of view." It was so; he realized it right away. He'd been following that crying so far and so long that he'd gotten into a different section of the country, and he'd gotten a different view, a terribly different view, and he never went back.

It is your face, O Lord, that I seek;
hide not your face.   –Psalm 27:8-9

DIFFERENT KINDS OF BUNDLES

ONCE there were a lot of folks, and every single one of them had bundles on their backs. But the bundles were all different. And these folks all belonged to one person who they called the Head Man. They were his folks and no one else's, and he had the whole say and could do anything he wanted to. But he was real nice and always did just the best thing, yes the best thing, whatever folks might say against it.

Well, about these folks with the different kinds of bundles on their backs. It was this way. One was a man with a real hefty bundle on his back that he'd put there himself, not all at once, but a little bit at a time for many years. It was a real odd bundle, made up of little things in the road that had got in his way or hurt him or put him back. Some of them were just little stones that had hurt his feet, and some were little stinging weeds that smarted him when he went by, and some were just bits of dirt someone had thrown at him, not meaning any great harm. He'd picked them all up, every worrying, prickly, hurting little thing, and he had piled them all on his back until he had a big bundle that he always carried about and never forgot for a minute.

He was forever looking out for such troubling things, and he would see them way ahead of him on the road, and sometimes he would think he saw them when there weren't any there at all. And instead of letting them lay where they were and going ahead and forgetting them, he would pick up every single one of them and pile them on that bundle

129

of his and carry them wherever he went. And he was always talking about them to folks, pointing out that little stone that he'd stubbed his toe on, this pesky weed that stung him, and the bit of mud somebody threw at him. He fretted and scolded and complained about them, and talked as if nobody else ever had so many trying things getting in his way as he had. He never took into account that he'd picked them up himself and piled them on his own back. If he had just let them lay and gone along, he'd have forgotten them all after a spell.

Then there was another man with a curious bundle, for it was all made out of money, dreadfully heavy and cold and hard to carry. Every speck of money he could scrape together he had put in that bundle until he could scarcely lift it, it was that big and weighed so much. He had plenty of chances to make it lighter, for there were folks all along the road that needed it badly, little children that had no clothes or food, and sick and old folks, everyone of them needing money urgently. But the man never gave them a bit. He kept it all on his back, hurting and weighing him down.

Then there was another man. He had a bundle that he didn't put on his back himself, and the Head Man didn't either. Folks did it to him. He hadn't done anything to deserve it, it was just put on him by other people, and so it was very hard to bear. But the Head Man had provided particularly for folks like that, and he'd said in public so everyone knew, that he'd help them carry such bundles himself, or maybe take them off if it seemed best. But this man didn't remember that. Or worse still, perhaps he didn't exactly believe it. So he went along all scrunched down with that hefty bundle other folks had piled up on him, not scolding or complaining or getting mad about it, but just thinking it had to be and that nobody could help him. But you see, it didn't have to be, and somebody could have helped him.

And then by and by along came a man who had such a hefty, hefty bundle. It was right between his shoulders, and it sort of scrooched him down, and it hurt him in his back and in his feelings. The Head Man had put that bundle on the man himself when he was a little bit of a fellow. He'd made it out of flesh and skin and things. It was just exactly like the man's body, so that when it ached he ached himself. And he'd had to carry that thing about all his born days.

I don't know why the Head Man did it, but I know how good and pleasant he was, and how he liked his folks and meant well to them, and how he knew just what ought to be and what ought not to be, so it stands to reason he'd done this thing on purpose, and not carelessly, and he hadn't made a mistake.

I've guessed a lot of reasons why he did it. Maybe he saw the man wouldn't have done so well without the bundle, might have run off, way off from the Head Man and the work he had to do. Or again, perhaps he wanted to make an example of the man, and show folks how patient and nice a person could be even though he had a hefty bundle to carry all his born days, one made out of flesh and skin and things, and that hurt dreadfully. But my other guess is the one I believe in most, that the Head Man did it to scrooch him down, so he would take notice of little tiny things down below that most folks never see, things that need him to watch them and do for them and tell about them. That's my favorite guess. At any rate the Head Man did right, I'm sure of that.

And it had made the man nicer and pleasant-spoken and kinder to folks, and especially to creatures. It had made him sort of bend down, it was so hefty, and so he'd had to take notice of teeny little things nobody else would scarcely see, tiny posies, and cunning little bugs, and creeping crawling things. He took a lot of comfort in them. And he told other folks about those little things and their little ways, and what they were made for, and things they could teach us. And it was real interesting and did folks good too. And he was patient and good and uncomplaining. There were a lot more folks with bundles, but I'm only going to tell you about these four this time.

Well, come pay day, these folks all came up before the Head Man to be settled with. And first he called up the man with the bundle all made out of things that had pricked him and tripped him and scratched him and put him back on the road. And then he had up the man with the money weighing him down, the money he'd kept away from poor folks and piled on his own back. And then came the fellow carrying the heavy bundle folks had put on him when it wasn't any fault of his own, and that he might have got rid of a long spell back, if he'd only remembered what the Head Man had said about such cases and how they could be helped.

I'm not going to tell you what he said to those folks, because it's none of my business. Whether he punished or scolded them, or sent them off to try again or what, never mind. Knowing as much as I do about the Head Man, I bet he made them feel terribly ashamed anyway.

But when he came to the man with the bundle made out of flesh and skin and things, he looked at him a minute and then he said, "Why, that's my own work! I made that bundle, and I fixed it on your back all myself. I hefted it and sized it, and I hefted you and sized you. A mite of a young one you were then. I made it just hefty enough for you to carry, not a bit heavier, no more or less. I remember it well. I haven't forgotten it. I never forgot it one minute since I fitted it on, though maybe you kind of thought by spells that I had. And now," he said—no, I can't tell you what he said—it's a secret. But I don't mind letting you know that the man was satisfied, perfectly satisfied. An angel told me he was, and he went on to say the man was wonderfully pleased to find he'd been wearing a bundle that the Head Man himself had made and fixed on him, hefting it and sizing it, and hefting him and sizing him too, so it wasn't too much for him to carry. But he isn't carrying it any more. The angel said so.

Come to me, all of you who are tired from carrying your heavy load, and I will give you rest. —Matthew 11:28

THE BOY WHO WAS
SCARED OF DYING

ONCE there was a boy who was dreadfully afraid of dying. Some folks are, you know. They've never done it to know how it feels, and they're scared. And this boy was that way. He wasn't very rugged, his health was sort of slim, and maybe that made him think about such things more. At any rate, he was terribly afraid of dying.

One day as this boy was sitting under a tree crying, he heard a little bit of a voice—not squeaky, but small and thin and soft—and he saw it was a flower talking, and it said, "What are you crying for?" And the boy said, "Because I'm scared of dying." Well, the flower just laughed, the most curious little pinky-white laugh, and it said, "Dying! Scared of dying? Why, I die myself every single year of my life." "Die yourself!" said the boy, "you're fooling. You're alive this minute." "Of course I am," said the flower. "But that's neither here nor there, I've died every year since I can remember." "Doesn't it hurt?" asked the boy. "No, it doesn't," said the flower. "It's real nice. You see, you get kind of tired holding your head up straight and looking pert and wide awake, and tired of the sun shining so hot, and the wind blowing you to pieces, and bees taking your honey. So it's nice to feel sleepy and kind of hang your head down, and get sleepier and sleepier, and then find you're dropping off. Then you wake up just at the nicest time of year, and come up and look around and—why, I like to die, I do." But somehow that didn't help the boy as much as you'd think. "I'm not a flower," he thought, "and maybe I wouldn't come up."

Well, another time he was sitting on a stone in the pasture, crying again, and he heard another unusual little voice. It wasn't like the flower's voice, but it was a little, woolly, soft fuzzy voice, and he saw it was a caterpillar talking to him. And the caterpillar said in his fuzzy little voice, "What are you crying for?" The boy answered, "I'm dreadfully afraid of dying, that's why." And the fuzzy caterpillar laughed and said, "Dying! I'm looking forward to dying myself. All my family die every once in awhile, and when they wake up they're just splendid, they've got wings, and the most wonderful colors, and they fly about and live on honey and things. Why, I wouldn't miss it for anything! I'm looking forward to it." But somehow that didn't cheer up the boy much. "I'm not a caterpillar," he thought, "and maybe I wouldn't wake up at all."

Well, there were lots of other things that talked to the boy and tried to help him, trees and flowers and grass and crawling things, that were always dying and living, and living and dying. The boy thought it didn't help him any, but I guess it did a little, for he couldn't help thinking of what they all said to him. But he was scared all the same.

Then one summer he began to fail faster and faster, and got so tired he could hardly hold his head up, but he was afraid all the same. And one day he was lying on the bed and looking out the east window, and the sun kept shining in his eyes till he shut them, and he fell asleep. He had a real good nap, and when he woke up he felt better and went out to take a walk.

And he began to think of what the flowers and trees and creatures had said about dying, and how they laughed at his being afraid of it, and he said to himself, "Well,

somehow I don't feel so scared today, but I suppose I am."
And just then what do you think happened? Why, he met
an angel. He'd never seen one before, but he knew it right
off. And the angel said, "Aren't you happy, little boy?"
And the boy said, "Well, I would be, only I'm so
frightfully scared of dying. It must be terribly curious to be
dead." And the angel said, "Why, you are dead." And he
was.

He will wipe away every tear from their eyes,
and death shall be no more.   –Rev. 21:4

PART 4

BARTHOLOMEW, THE FRIENDLY SCARECROW

WHEN Mr. Jones tried to plant his garden one spring morning not so long ago, he ran into some trouble from a flock of hungry blackbirds. As fast as he would put in a row of corn, the birds would swoop down and gobble it up. "I just don't know what to do about those hungry blackbirds," the farmer said to his wife that afternoon when he went back to the house for dinner. "I have an idea," his wife replied, "let's make a scarecrow to help keep them away." "That's a good idea," said the farmer. "I don't know why I didn't think of it before."

Mrs. Jones gathered together a pair of Mr. Jones' patched blue jeans, a threadbare shirt, and a tattered jacket. Then she got a pair of his old worn-out work shoes. Mr. Jones brought a burlap feed bag, some straw, and a long wooden pole from the barn. Mrs. Jones went to her sewing basket and returned with a needle, some heavy thread, and two brass buttons. She carefully sewed the buttons on the burlap bag for the eyes, and she stitched a big friendly smile on it. She stuffed the feed bag, the shirt, and the blue jeans with straw.

When she had finished, they hung the scarecrow on the long wooden pole in a prominent place overlooking the cornfield. Mrs. Jones looked at their scarecrow and said, "Frank, our scarecrow needs a hat if he is to look respectable, and you've been needing a new hat yourself." Then she took his hat and placed it on the scarecrow's head. As she did, a gust of wind kicked up and the scarecrow almost seemed to come to life. "Let's call him Bartholomew," they decided.

Bartholomew was a friendly scarecrow, much too friendly to keep the blackbirds away for long. They were afraid at first and stayed away, but then Bartholomew waved at them and greeted them with a smile. He was new and not quite sure of his job. "Well," said the leader of the flock, "this fellow is all right. Mr. Jones always shakes his fists and chases us away when we come to dinner." So the birds flew over and perched on Bartholomew's shoulders. One even landed on his hat. Bartholomew didn't mind a bit. He enjoyed the company. The birds laughed and talked and had a feast.

Soon Mr. Jones came shaking his fists, and the birds flew off. "Bartholomew, Bartholomew, Bartholomew," the farmer said, "you're supposed to keep those pesky blackbirds away. We need the corn to feed the farm animals when winter comes." Bartholomew was sad. The blackbirds were his friends. Then he had an idea.

When the crows returned, Bartholomew told them why Mr. Jones needed the corn. "Wait until fall," he said. "Then there will be plenty of corn for all of us. Why not try Mr. Green's garden down the road." The birds liked Bartholomew, so they listened to him. They flew by to chat with the friendly scarecrow, but they didn't bother the cornfield any more that season. "Bartholomew is certainly doing a fine job watching over the cornfield," said the farmer to his wife as they were feeding the chickens. She agreed.

Soon all of the animals on the farm heard about Bartholomew and went to visit him. Hilda the hen and her chicks, Bossie the cow, and old Nellie the plowhorse, came to say hello. Hector and Herman, farmer Jones' two prize-winning pigs, stopped by to greet the scarecrow. At no time, however, was Bartholomew more surprised than when he looked down to see William, the goat, nibbling on his shoe. "Billy," said Bartholomew, "I think you would like that corn much better." "You're right," said the goat as he sampled an ear. Farmer Jones came with a rope to lead him away.

Scruffy, the family cat, stopped to visit just long enough to spot a field mouse hiding in some tall grass at the edge of the cornfield. "Meow. You have your job, I have mine," the old cat said. "I'll see you later." The mouse scurried off. Scruffy raced after him in hot pursuit. Betty Beagle, the Joneses' dog, and her three puppies, Rover, Fido, and Spot, came to visit Bartholomew.

The scarecrow grew especially fond of Spot. He enjoyed the puppy's frequent visits. He liked watching the little fellow chase his tail, and play with the laces that dangled from the scarecrow's heavy worn work shoes. The pup visited Bartholomew almost every day, and the summer seemed to pass quickly. The corn grew tall. It was nearing harvest time.

Then one day as Spot was visiting the old scarecrow, it started to rain. The little dog darted into the barn for shelter. The sky grew black. The wind blew. There was a crack of thunder and then another. The rain poured down.

"Crack!" A bolt of lightning struck the barn. It burst instantly into flames. Thick black smoke rolled out to meet the sky. Mr. Jones saw the lightning strike, and rushed into the burning building to rescue the animals. Out he came with Bossie the cow and Nellie the horse. They were safe, but the farmer hadn't seen Spot go into the barn.

"There's no time to waste," thought Bartholomew, "I must act quickly." The scarecrow leaped from his pole, and dashed into the blazing barn after the puppy. "Spot!"

he called out. The puppy was frightened, unable to move. "Over here," called the courageous scarecrow. Spot heard him. At last he could see the way out of the burning structure. He darted out to safety.

Bartholomew turned to go out of the barn behind him, but a flaming beam came crashing down, pinning him to the floor. Mr. Jones picked up the frightened puppy. He stroked Spot's head, watching helplessly as the barn burned to the ground. When the flames died down, all they could find of the brave scarecrow were two brass buttons in the ashes.

Mr. Jones with help from his neighbors built a new barn, and harvested the corn. Thanks to Bartholomew, it was the largest harvest in years. They would miss the friendly scarecrow.

Winter came. It was cold. The snow was deep. Mr. Jones and some of the other farmers worried that the deer and other wild animals would starve without help. They loaded their sleds with corn and hay, and took it back into the woods where the animals could find it. The animals were saved. Mrs. Jones fed the birds from a birdfeeder in their yard. Winter passed into spring.

"It's time to put in the garden," said the farmer to his wife. "It won't be the same without old Bartholomew though." The blackbirds were as hungry as ever. There were new ones, young birds that hadn't met Bartholomew, young ones to whom the dashing scarecrow would be just a legend. The farmer and his wife decided to make another scarecrow. Of course, he would never be the same as Bartholomew.

Mrs. Jones gathered together a pair of Mr. Jones' patched blue jeans, a threadbare shirt, and a tattered jacket. Then she located a pair of his old worn-out work shoes. Mr. Jones brought a burlap feed bag, some straw, and a long wooden pole from the barn. Mrs. Jones stuffed the burlap feed bag, the shirt, and the blue jeans with the straw. She went for her sewing basket and returned with a needle, some heavy thread, and the two brass buttons she had rescued from the ashes of that terrible fire. She carefully sewed the buttons on the burlap bag for the eyes, and she stitched a big friendly smile on it.

When she finished they hung the scarecrow on the long wooden pole in a prominent place overlooking the cornfield. Mrs. Jones looked at their scarecrow, then she took her husband's hat and placed it on his head. They started to walk back to the house for supper. "Thank you," said a friendly voice behind them. They turned around to look, and smiled. It was the scarecrow grinning from ear to ear. "You really do need a hat out in the hot sun," he said. Bartholomew was back.

THE LITTLE YELLOW CAB

O N a crisp, cool, autumn morning not so very long ago, a tiny yellow car rolled off the assembly line of a factory in the motor city, for that is where little cars are born. It was easy to see it was something special. It's hard to say for certain why. Maybe it was the cheerful chatter of her tiny engine. Perhaps it was her friendly honk.

The little car was taken on a tractor trailer, along with some of her sisters, to an automobile dealer in a small town not very far, perhaps, from where you live. There they were taken into a brightly lit, colorfully decorated showroom. Many people came to admire the cars. First came a school teacher. She picked a flashy red car. Then came a farmer. He purchased a little green pick-up truck. Next came the plumber. He chose a blue panel truck.

The little car waited patiently in the salesroom. One day a man, a boy named Billy, and a dog named Spot came to the showroom. "Hello," greeted the salesman with a friendly smile. "What can I do for you today?" "I would like to try out that little car," the man said. Spot just wagged his tail and barked. So the salesman took them for a test drive in the yellow car. "I'll take it," said the man. "This is a good car." So he bought it, and they drove home in the little yellow car.

The man took good care of the tiny automobile. He washed it and waxed it. He tended to every rattle and squeak, and the little car was very happy. He drove her back and forth to his job at the steel mill everyday. At night he kept her in his warm garage. Billy wished he

could drive the little car, but his Dad said he would have to wait until he was older.

Every weekend the man took his family on short trips in his car. Spot went too. Sometimes they went to the farm to visit grandfather and grandmother. Sometimes they went to the zoo to visit the wild animals. Wherever they went in the little car, they had fun.

One day, however, the man decided it was time to trade the tiny car in, for it was too small for his growing family. So he drove the little car back to the place where he first bought her. "Our family has grown," he said, "so we need a larger car." The little yellow car was very sad. "Goodbye," she wanted to say, but all she could do was cry.

One of the salesmen parked the little car in the middle of his lot and there it sat for several weeks. Few people noticed the tiny automobile.

One morning, however, a heavy-set man in a black overcoat came to the little car. He kicked her tires, and slammed her doors. He opened the hood to check the engine and then he bought it and drove it home. He was hard on the little car. He rarely washed or waxed it. He seldom changed the oil. He drove it hard, scarcely slowing down for bumps and ruts in the road, until one day the little car just couldn't start.

"This car is a piece of junk," the fat man grumbled, and he drifted it into a field near his home and forgot about it. There the old car sat for several years through rain and snow. Children played in the old car and it didn't matter to them that the tires were flat and the seats were worn. It didn't seem to matter that there was a dent in the fender and a broken headlight. The car was happy here with the children.

But then the neighborhood parents started complaining about the old car. "It's dangerous," said Mrs. Jones. "It looks terrible, such an eyesore," said Mrs. Smith.

One day a tow truck drove up and two men jumped out. "There's the car. Mr. Jones said to move it out of here as soon as possible." The children watched as the men wrapped the tow chain around the car's tiny frame. It was a sad day for them. It had been a lot of fun playing in the old car. The little car shed a tear. "Goodbye," she said. "Goodbye," they waved. The tow truck rumbled away pulling the little car.

"Where am I going now?" the little car thought anxiously. The truck started down a long dusty road and before long the little yellow car had her answer. It was the scrapyard. The junkyard—the end of the line.

The tiny automobile saw row upon row of cars like herself. Some of them even looked familiar, and most were in a lot worse condition than herself. "What will become of me?" she wondered. The battered car next to her said, "We all end up here sooner or later. Don't worry, just enjoy the rest. We've earned it." The little car was only momentarily consoled by her new-found friend. It wasn't long before she was again worrying about what would happen to her. Day after day she waited.

She watched the men at work in the scrapyard. She saw them remove a door from an old red panel truck. She watched them take a bumper and fender from an aging blue convertible. "What will become of me?" she honked, as a tear streamed from her headlight. Then one day she heard one of the men say, "Yes, he wants to buy them all and cut them up and melt them down in his fiery blast furnaces to made new steel."

Suddenly the little yellow car knew what would happen. She was afraid and she cried and cried. "I don't

want to be melted down into new steel. I don't want to be a stove or a refrigerator or anything else. I just want to be me." The other cars tried to console her. "Don't worry," they said. "It will be a new life. We're looking forward to it." But the little car was not consoled.

Then a wonderful thing happened. One of the workers and the owner of the scrapyard came up to the little car, a dog behind them. Suddenly a flash of recognition came to the tiny car. "Isn't that little Billy and Spot? How he has grown!" She heard Billy say to the owner, "I'll give you fifty dollars for that old car. I want to fix it up." "It's a deal," said the owner. The little yellow car flashed her headlights and smiled.

The next day two men in a tow truck backed up to the little car and towed it away—to Bill's house. Bill worked on the little car in his garage at night after work. He gave her new tires and changed her oil. He tuned her tiny engine. He repaired her upholstery. He fixed the dent in her tiny fender and replaced her broken headlight. Finally he gave the old car a fresh coat of bright yellow paint. She felt like a new car again.

Bill drove the yellow car to work and back everyday. He parked her in his warm garage at night. Everyone who saw the little yellow car admired it. Bill and the little car just smiled.

One day, however, the owner of the scrapyard told Bill he was going to close. Bill was sad to lose his job. He looked everywhere for work, but jobs were hard to find. The little yellow car wanted to help Bill, but how?

Then Bill had an idea. And that is how the tiny car became the little yellow cab. She was very happy.

SACRAMENT

Oh, Love has made a sacrament
Of every single thing I do
Lighting candles in the dusk
Has a meaning sweet and new.

I find a gay significance
In placing roses in a vase,
In piling logs of fragrant pine
Beside the cozy chimney-place.

The polishing of kitchen-ware
Is very near a sacred rite,
And putting on their proper shelves
The cups and saucers gleaming bright.

There is a gentle dignity
In cutting loaves of smooth, new bread,
In folding linen, fresh and clean,
And faintly scented, for my bed.

Our humble home becomes a shrine
With windows seeking heaven's blue,
For Love has made a sacrament
Of every single thing I do.

- Elsie S. Fischer